MOSCOW KREMLIN

State Museum-Preserve of History and Culture

THE ARMOURY

A Guide

D0982161

Red Square

Moscow 1995

Moscow Kremlin

State

THE ARMOURY

Museum-Preserve

of History and Culture

V.S. Goncharenko and V.I. Narozhnaya

A Guide

Cover:
Gospel. Moscow, first half of 17th century (□37)

Text: V.S.Goncharenko and V.I.Narozhnaya
Translation: Kathleen Cook-Horujy
Editor: V.F.Petrov
Photographs: N.N.Alexeyev
              N.N.Rakhmanov
              A.V.Sverdlov
              V.N.Seregin
Design: N.I.Kalinin

Computer-aided makeup A.V.Kosenyuk
Fonts: Newton, Pragmatica
Red Square Publishers,
109147 Moscow, Vorontsovskaya, 23
Printing: Brepols, Belgium

ISBN 5-88678-030-0
ISBN 5-900743-16-0

If you enter the grounds of the Moscow Kremlin through Borovitsky Gate the first building that you notice on your left is the Armoury Museum. In the architectural ensemble of the Kremlin, which combines the styles of many epochs from mediaeval times to the present day in perfect harmony, the Armoury occupies a worthy place. It was designed and built under the supervision of the architect Academician Konstantin Andreyevich Ton as part of the grandiose construction complex of the Grand Kremlin Palace (1830–1849), the Moscow residence of the Russian tsars.

Completed in 1851 and specially designed as a museum, the building is most palatial. Its elegant yet majestic forms, from the general view to the splendid interiors of the vestibule, the grand staircase of white marble and the suites of nine magnificent halls constitute a fine specimen of Russian architecture of the mid-19th century. And behind its massive doors lies a rich and fascinating world of artistic treasures.

The State Armoury, one of Russia's oldest museums, has almost five hundred years of history and its unique collection of decorative and applied art is closely linked with the history of the Moscow Kremlin itself. The museum's collection was formed gradually over several centuries.

The first reference in ancient documents to the Moscow Kremlin's Armoury as a royal treasure house dates back to 1508. The basis of the collection consists of treasures from the Kremlin repositories: gold- and silverware, weapons and horse harness, ancient state regalia, ceremonial dress, mediaeval Russian embroidery and other works of art fashioned in the Armoury (hence the name of the future museum), the Gold, Silver and Tsarina's chambers, and the workshops of the Stables Office in the Moscow Kremlin, where the finest armourers, engravers, enamellers, silversmiths, jewellers and icon-painters worked, drawn from all the great centres of mediaeval Russia – Vladimir, Suzdal, Kostroma, Rostov, Novgorod and so on.

Nothing is here by chance or lacks artistic value. All the museum's exhibits are true works of art which have immortalised the skill, taste and imagination of generations of Russian craftsmen. The collection is an eloquent testimony to the talent and giftedness of the Russian people, their feeling for beauty and ability to create it.

The lovingly preserved items of West-European and Oriental art bear witness to Russian appreciation of and respect for the art of other peo-

ples. Purchased or presented as ambassadorial gifts, many of them are artistic masterpieces. And again one is amazed by their variety: from precious fabrics and silverware to a unique collection of carriages.

The late 18th and early 19th centuries were a time when the royal and imperial treasuries of Europe, and also some private collections, were

turned into museum collections, such as the Louvre in Paris, the Prado in Madrid, the National Gallery in London, the museums in Vienna, etc. The formation of museums in Russia kept pace with the process in the rest of Europe. The priceless historical and artistic treasures of the Moscow Kremlin were collected into a single repository on the basis of which the Armoury Museum was set up in 1806. This collection soon outgrew the framework of a palace museum and acquired the significance of a national artistic heritage.

Today the museum's life reflects the desire of our society to preserve the past, the monuments of our history. The ancient treasures of the Moscow Kremlin have been proclaimed the national property of the peoples of Russia. In recognition of the uniqueness of the monuments in the Moscow Kremlin and their exceptional place in the development of world culture, UNESCO has placed them under special preservation as part of mankind's historical and artistic heritage.

The latest reconstruction of the various halls and exhibits of the Armoury took place in 1983–1986. The aim of this guide is to introduce you to these exhibits.

We trust that this introduction to the masterpieces in the Armoury Museum will be both enjoyable and instructive for all our visitors.

IRINA RODIMTSEVA
*Director of the Moscow Kremlin
State Museum-Preserve
of History and Culture*

*The Armoury.
Grand staircase*

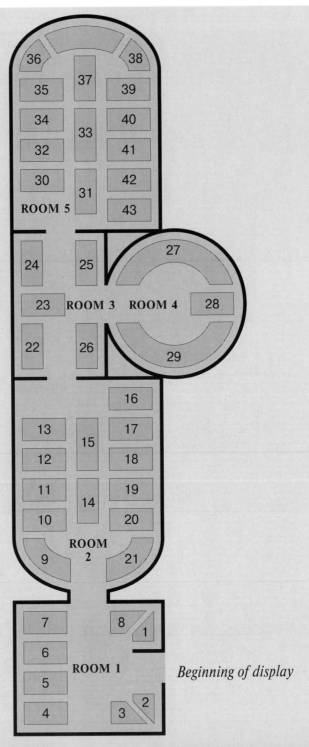

Beginning of display

FIRST FLOOR *Beginning of display*

ROOM 1 Showcases 1 to 8

RUSSIAN GOLD AND SILVERWARE
OF THE 12TH
TO 17TH CENTURIES

page 14

ROOM 2 Showcases 9 to 21

RUSSIAN GOLD AND SILVERWARE
OF THE 17TH
TO EARLY 20TH CENTURIES

page 48

ROOM 3 Showcases 22 to 26

ORIENTAL AND EUROPEAN
CEREMONIAL WEAPONS
OF THE 15TH TO 19TH CENTURIES

page 134

ROOM 4 Showcases 27 to 29

RUSSIAN ARMS
OF THE 12TH
TO EARLY 19TH CENTURIES

page 118

ROOM 5 Showcases 30 to 43

WEST EUROPEAN SILVER
OF THE 13TH TO
19TH CENTURIES

page 146

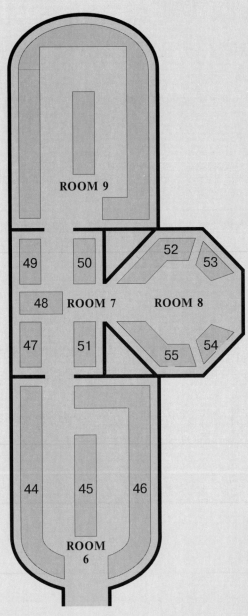

Continuation of display

GROUND FLOOR *Continuation of display*

ROOM 6 Showcases 44 to 46

PRECIOUS FABRICS, PICTORIAL AND ORNAMENTAL EMBROI-
DERY OF THE 14TH TO 18TH CENTURIES, RUSSIAN SECULAR
DRESS OF THE 16TH TO EARLY 20TH CENTURIES
page 202

ROOM 7 Showcases 47 to 51

ANCIENT STATE REGALIA
AND CEREMONIAL OBJECTS
OF THE 13TH TO 18TH CENTURIES
page 244

ROOM 8 Showcases 52 to 55

HORSE HARNESS
OF THE 16TH TO 18TH CENTURIES
page 260

ROOM 9

CARRIAGES OF THE 16TH
TO 18TH CENTURIES
page 272

FIRST FLOOR *Beginning of display*

ROOM 1 — RUSSIAN GOLD AND SILVERWARE OF THE 12TH TO 17TH CENTURIES

The State Armoury Museum is a kind of encyclopaedia of Russian art and Russian history. Most of the items on display here were actually made on the territory of the Moscow Kremlin, in the workshops that served the grand princes and tsars.

Many of the works by highly skilled masters which are kept in the Armoury are connected with the names of famous figures in Russian history, and some pieces are mentioned in documents dating back to the 14th century as symbols of the power of the grand princes and the Russian state.

The Armoury collection, the only one of its kind in Russia, enables you to form a clear picture of the exceptional mastery of Russian gold- and silversmiths. From the unique objects in this collection you can trace the development of Russian decorative and applied art and learn about the different methods of working precious metals.

The items exhibited in the first two rooms on the first floor are for the most part the work of Moscow Kremlin masters, but here you will also find specimens of jewellery from other famous cities, such as Kiev, Novgorod, Yaroslavl, Kostroma, Chernigov, Ryazan and also works of Byzantine, Southern Slav and Georgian applied art which help one to understand the origins and interaction of Russian mediaeval art.

Showcase 1

WORKS FROM BYZANTIUM, SERBIA AND GEORGIA

The Armoury has a small, but extremely valuable collection of Byzantine art covering a period of almost one thousand years from the 5th to the 15th century. The artistic culture of Byzantium, after absorbing the heritage of the antique world and the ancient Orient, developed a style of its own.

Trading and diplomatic relations between Old Russia and Byzantium developed as early as the 10th century. The items displayed in this case were most likely brought to Russia by merchants and diplomats. The Armoury's collection of Byzantine art includes items of gold and silver, cloisonné enamel, stone carving, textiles and embroidery of the 14th and 15th centuries. The silver-gilt jug from the Sudzha trove in the vicinity of Kursk dates back to the late 4th and early 5th centuries and was found in the grave of a pagan prince. The jug is decorated with chasing and the figures of the

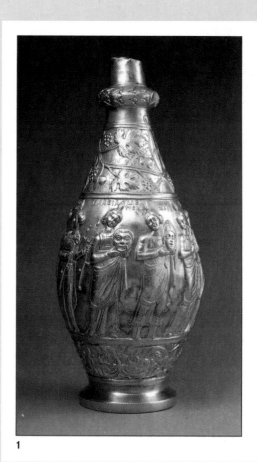

1

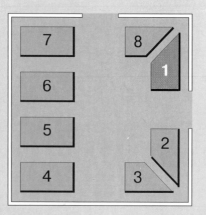

nine Muses. You have probably noticed that the influence of antique art is felt strongly in the figures and ornament.

The Armoury possesses one of the finest collections of cameos by Byzantine masters of the 11th and 12th centuries. They are small icons with the carved figures of saints on agate, jasper, lapis-

zuli, steatite and chrysoprase. The
rticles of steatite and other soft varie-
es of stone remind one strongly of
ory carving. For example, the 11th-
entury icon of the holy warrior St
emetrius of Salonica on horseback
rved in steatite. In spite of the icon's
nall dimensions, the figure of the
int with a sword in his hand is very
npressive and reminiscent of ancient
questrian statues. Legend has it that
is icon was sent to Prince Dmitry
onskoy by the Byzantine Emperor in
onour of the victory at Kulikovo Field
n 8 September, 1380, which marked
e beginning of Russia's liberation
om Mongol-Tartar dominion.

2

3

□ 1. *Jug from Sudzha trove.* Constantinople, c. 400. Silver; chasing, gilding. Height 38.5
□ 2. *Cameo of Christ Blessing.* Byzantine, 11th century. Jasper, gold, gems; carving. Height 12, width 8.2
□ 3. *Icon of St Demetrius of Salonica.* Byzantium, 11th–14th centuries. Steatite, silver; carving, chasing, gilding. Height 31.4, width 26.4

The 11th and 12th centuries witnessed the flowering of Byzantine art. By this time Constantinople was a major artistic centre and the articles fashioned by its craftsmen were exported to Western Europe, the Orient and Old Russia.

It was in Constantinople that the fine art of cloisonné enamel first saw the light of day. The case contains several items decorated with cloisonné enamel: a small 11th-century oval-shaped icon of the Crucifixion made of gold and found in the Ryazan trove in 1822, the plates on the cover of the icon of Our Lady of Compassion (12th–13th century) and the gold icon-reliquary of the Descent into Hell (l2th–13th century). Byzantine cloisonné enamel was famed for its high quality, fine workmanship and harmonic colour combinations. It was used to decorate clothing, goblets, dishes and church plate. It had a great influence on the development of enamelwork in many other countries, including Kievan Russia.

Byzantine silversmiths are represented by a 12th-century staurotechos or cross-holder (top, left) brought by Metropolitan Alexis to Grand Prince Ivan II in 1354 from Patriarch Philotheos. The cross-holder was greatly prized by the princes of Moscow who used it to bless their eldest son, a fact mentioned in their wills.

4

5

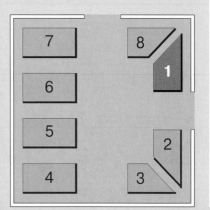

**4. Icon-reli-
ary of the De-
ent Into Hell.**
zantium, 12th
ntury. Gold;
isonné enam-
Height 9.5,
th 8.5
**5. Staurote-
os.** Byzantium,
th century. Sil-
, wood; chas-
. Height 20.5,
th 17
**6. Helmet
th Deisis.** By-
ntium, 13th
ntury. Iron with
er and gold
bossing.
ight 30

6

e case contains a tall, conical-
aped helmet, known as a "Yerikhon-
". It is made of a single sheet of iron
d decorated with fine silver foliate
nbossing. Around the broad lower
nd of the helmet are half-figures of
e Deisis tier: Christ, the Virgin Mary,
e archangels Michael and Gabriel

and two seraphim. This helmet was already mentioned among the objects in
the Grand Royal Treasury in 1687. It
was probably brought from Byzantium
by merchants.
Here too you can see works of art from
Serbia and Georgia which bear the
mark of Byzantine influence.

Showcase 2

RUSSIAN GOLD AND SILVERWARE OF THE 12TH TO 15TH CENTURIES

The thousand years of Byzantine art played a major role in world artistic culture. The importance of Byzantium was particular great for early Russian art. Yet in spite of the strong Byzantine influence, Russian masters succeeded in preserving originality and national character in their works.

Unfortunately very few items relating to the early period of the Russian state have survived. Some of them were destroyed during the years of internecine wars between the princes, others during the frequent fires. The Mongol invasion dealt a particularly severe blow to Russian art. During this period many artistic techniques were lost. Nevertheless individual items have survived which testify to the high level of the Russian jeweller's art.

Here you will find specimens of the earliest work by Russian craftsmen, dating back to the 13th to 15th centuries. There was no centralised Russian state during this period. Russia was di-

7

8

□ **7–8. Kolt medallion (front and back).** *Old Russia, Ryazan, 12th century. Gold, pearls, gems; cloisonné enamel, filigree, seeds of gold. Diameter 12.5*

□ **9. Humerals from Ryazan trove.** *Old Russia,
Ryazan, 12th century. Gold, gems, pearls;
cloisonné enamel, filigree, seeds of gold. Diameter
of medallions from 7.5 to 12.5*

vided into separate principalities, many of which were not only political and economic, but also cultural centres of the Russian land.

Most of the articles here were made in the principalities of Vladimir-Suzdal, Ryazan and Chernigov. It was from these places that the finest painters and craftsmen flocked to Moscow, which later became the capital of the centralised Russian state, and created splendid works of art reflecting the national traditions that had grown up over the centuries. Their work is marked by a simplicity, restraint and precision of form which lend a special monumentality to all types of art of that period.

Treasures of the 12th and 13th centuries have survived from the Ryazan trove, a monument of the art of jewellery in pre-Mongol Russia, which was discovered near the village of Old Ryazan in 1822. They include a royal humeral (an insignia worn by the grand princes and tsars), *kolts* (medallions attached to a female headdress), earrings, signet rings, bracelets, etc.

The abundance of precious stones adorning the big round medallions, the many colours and the widespread use of filigree (patterns made of smooth or twisted gold, silver or copper wire which are either openwork or soldered

10

11

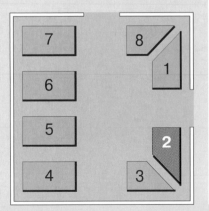

□**10. *Star-shaped kolt medallion from Tula trove.*** *Old Russia, 12th century. Silver, casting; filigree, seeds of gold. Height (without attached pendant) 11, width 10*
□**11. *Chalice.*** *Old Russia, 12th century. Silver; chasing, carving, gilding. Height 26.*
Donated by Prince Yuri Dolgoruky (?) to the Cathedral of the Transfiguration in the town of Pereslavl-Zalessky

□ **12. Bowl.** *Old Russia, Chernigov, 12th century. Silver; forging, carving. Height 9.8, diameter 34. Belonged to Prince Vladimir of Chernigov*

a metal base), are all characteristic
tures of the Old Ryazan school of
sters. Articles like these have not
n found in any other Russian town.
e figures of saints on the medallions
executed in the technique of
isonné enamel.

amel is a vitreous paste which takes
different colours from the addition
oxides. It is applied to small cloisons
cells, formed by fine strips of gold
ch are soldered on sideways to a
tern already applied. The process of
king cloisonné enamel was very
nplicated and demanded considera-
skill and experience. Cloisonné
mel represents the flowering of me-
eval Russian jewellery-making in
pre-Mongol period.

re too are pendants for a female
ddress. The surface of the star-
ped medallion (*kolt*) from the Tula
e (12th–13th century) is decorated
n five thousand minute seeds of
d, each of which is surrounded by a
gree band.

12th-century silver chalice is a
specimen of applied art by masters

in the principality of Vladimir-Suzdal.
On the smooth forged bowl of the
chalice you can see carved figures of
saints in gilded medallions. Note how
well the master has balanced the proportions of the different sections, the
bowl, stem and base. This chalice was
commissioned by Yuri Dolgoruky,
Prince of Vladimir-Suzdal and Grand
Prince of Kiev for presentation to the
Cathedral of the Transfiguration in
Pereslavl-Zalessky.

The big silver bowl which belonged to
Prince Vladimir of Chernigov is an interesting example of 12th-century domestic silverware. It is simple in form,
the only decoration being the carved
inscription round the rim. From early
times Russian masters made use of inscriptions as ornament, arranging
them in bands, circles or rings. The
size of the bowl and inscription suggest
that it was used as a loving cup.

The thirteenth century and first half of
the fourteenth are generally regarded
as a "fallow" period in Russian art due
to the Mongol invasion. Very few
works have survived from this time.

They are mostly small crosses, icons or icon mounts carved from wood, stone or ivory.

A special place in the culture of mediaeval Russia belongs to the art of Novgorod the Great, an important centre of arts and crafts in the north which, like Pskov, escaped the horrors of the Mongol invasion.

We could say that silver-work in Novgorod was born at the same time as the city itself. The first workshops appeared at the beginning of the 12th century, probably attached to the Cathedral of St Sophia, and existed until the end of the 17th century. Novgorodian applied art retained its distinctive features for several centuries. The silverware made by Novgorodian masters is laconic and expressive. Novgorodian jewellers made skilful use of such techniques as filigree, chasing, damascening, enamelling, etc.

The early Novgorodian items include the small steatite icon of St Nicholas (13th–14th cent.) and the icon of Christ Enthroned with SS Simeon and Juliana (12th cent.). Wood was often used as a material for small plastic articles. The folding icon of the Crucifixion with Attendant Figures (late 15th cent.) and also the composition of the Exaltation of the Virgin on the 15th-century icon from the Annunciation

13

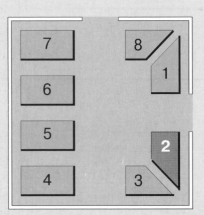

Cathedral of the Moscow Kremlin are masterpieces of Novgorodian woodcarving.

The Armoury contains many unique articles wrought by Novgorod the Great's talented craftsmen.

One of the earliest specimens is a jasper chalice mounted in silver filigree with precious stones. It was made for Archbishop Moses of Novgorod in 1329, as can be seen from the carved inscription round the rim of the cup. Note how cleverly the master com-

☐ **13. Chalice.**
Russia,
Novgorod, 1329.
Jasper, silver,
gems; carving,
filigree, gilding.
Height 23.2
☐ **14. Icon of**
the Exaltation of
the Virgin. *Carv-*
ing – Russia,
Novgorod (?),
15th century,
Mount – Moscow,
15th century.
Wood, gold,
gems; filigree
carving. Height
with head-piece
13.7, width 9.2

es the red jasper with the filigree
carving.

ornament reminds one of the
ided patterns in 14th-century
gorodian manuscript books. The
ree is arranged in short spirals of
silver threads placed side by side.
chalice is expressive, simple and
ndid.

ew form of gold and silver drinking
el saw the light of day in
gorod, namely the kovsh or dipper.
the earliest surviving silver dippers
connected with Novgorod in some
The oldest in the Armoury collec-

tion is a small smooth dipper with a
pointed, turned-up lip and a small oval
peliust (the curved end of the handle)
on a short thin neck, which first belonged to Archbishop Euthymius of
Novgorod (first half of 15th cent.) and
later to Ivan the Terrible's son, Ivan.
This dipper is very close to its wooden
prototype.

The reliquary (mid-14th cent.) with
figures of saints which remind one of
the compositions on the famous doors
of the Trinity Cathedral in the town of
Alexandrov is a specimen of Tverian
art.

15

In the fourteenth century Nizhny Novgorod acquired political influence. It was during this period, in 1383, that the reliquary for holding the sacred relics brought from Constantinople by Archbishop Dionysius of Suzdal at the request of Prince Dmitry of Nizhny Novgorod was made. The reliquary is made of silver in the shape of a quatrefoil. It is adorned with black and dark-green enamel on the selected metal background. In the little windows, under the mica, are the sacred relics which Dionysius brought from Constantinople. Just before Dionysius' second visit to Constantinople, during which he died, the reliquary was immured in the wall of the Cathedral of the Nativity in Suzdal, where it was discovered in 1401 and sent to the treasury of the Moscow princes. After that it was passed down from father to son with the other valuables in the grand prince's coffers.

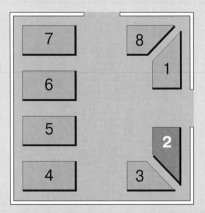

☐ **16. Reliquary.** *Russia, Suzdal (?), 1383. Silver, gems, mica; enamel, niello, carving. Height 39, width 39*

Showcase 3

MOSCOW JEWELLERY OF THE 15TH CENTURY

Already by the 15th century the work of Moscow masters was prized very highly indeed. This is explained largely by the fact that Russia had thrown off Mongol dominion and the Russian lands had united round a single centre – Moscow. The Moscow jewellers were skilled in the use of the various techniques for making articles of precious metals: chasing, niello, carving and casting. It was in the technique of filigree, however, that they attained exceptional mastery.

The gold cover on the Morozov Gospel is a rare specimen of applied art of this period. This parchment manuscript of the Gospels is thought to have been made in 1415 for the Assumption Cathedral of the Moscow Kremlin at the request of Metropolitan Photius. In the second half of the 17th century it was restored on the orders of the boyar B.I.Morozov (1590–1661). The cover is embellished with high-relief chasing depicting saints, dense and intricate

17

filigree ornament and uncut precious stones. The composition of the cover is unusual. There is nothing like it in the earlier period or in subsequent times. The execution of the coloured miniatures, headpieces and initials suggests that they were the work of artists from Andrei Rublev's circle.

There is another fine specimen of applied art from the Moscow principality here, namely, the cover for the famous icon of Our Lady of Vladimir (the icon itself, now in the Tretyakov Gallery is a Byzantine work of the late 11th – early

□ **17. Gospel.**
Moscow, beginning of 15th century. Gold, gems, pearls, parchment; chasing, filigree. Height 39, width 34
□ **18. Cover for icon of Our Lady of Vladimir.** *Moscow, late 14th – early 15th century. Gold, gems; chasing, stamping. Height 105, width 70*

18

h century). The museum possesses
ee covers for this icon. The earliest
stamped gold cover dating back to
early 15th century.
e technique of stamping the pattern
hand on a thin sheet of gold or sil-
appeared in Russia as early as the
h century and became very popular
1 Russian masters because it was
nomical in the use of metal and

simpler in technique than chasing.
Stamping was used to decorate icon
covers and book bindings.

The spoon-shaped dipper which belonged to Archbishop Jonah of
Novgorod and has the monogram
"Jonah" carved on the bottom in Russian with alternately gilded chased
spoons radiating from the centre, dates
back to the middle of the 15th century.

Showcase 4

MOSCOW JEWELLERY OF THE 15TH CENTURY

Note the cover for the manuscript Gospel dated 1499 in showcase 4. It was donated by Metropolitan Simon to the Assumption Cathedral. The masters have skilfully combined the techniques of casting, lacy filigree and pure, transparent enamel in this article.

The gold cover for the icon of Our Lady of Vladimir is a splendid example of 15th-century filigree work. The elegant pattern of the high-relief filigree on a smooth gold background alternates with chased representations of chrch festivals. In the upper section are the chased figures of Christ, the Virgin Mary, John the Baptist, the archangels and apostles. The cover was commissioned by Metropolitan Photius to mark his appointment as metropolitan of Moscow in 1410. If you look carefully at the filigree ornament in the lower section, you will see Photius' monogram written in Greek inside a circle. Photius, a Greek by birth, had

19

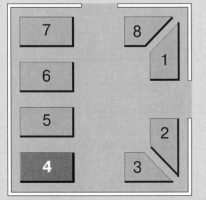

workshops in his Kremlin residence, where many visiting masters were invited and local traditions interacted with Byzantine ones. This resulted in the appearance of a number of splendid items of jewellery..

In 1486 two silver reliquaries commissioned by Ivan III were made for the Moscow Assumption Cathedral, which are known as the Great Zion and Small Zion. They were carried out during special religious services as symbols of the Church.

21

☐ **19. Gospel.** *Moscow, 1499. Silver, paper; chasing, casting, filigree, enamel, carving. Height 33, width 22*
☐ **20. Small Zion.** *Moscow, 1486. Copper; chasing, gilding, niello. Height 63*
☐ **21. Cover for icon of Our Lady of Vladimir.** *Moscow, first third of 15th century. Gold; chasing, filigree. Length 105, width 70*

Showcase 5

THE ART OF THE MOSCOW GOLDSMITHS IN THE 16TH CENTUR

The flowering of jewellery-making in Russia came in the 16th century. By then Moscow was the centre of the young state's cultural life. The rapid growth of Moscow's political and economic might demanded fitting expression. In 1547 Grand Prince Ivan the Terrible of All Russia assumed the title of tsar, and from then onwards the Moscow tsar's processions, receptions and banquets acquired a special sumptuousness. The finest jewellers, armourers, saddlers and carriage-makers were invited to the Kremlin workshops.

The articles produced by Moscow jewellers during this period are marked by a refined simplicity, logic of form and elegance of austere and precise ornament.

In the 16th century the technique of niello work became highly developed in Russia. Niello is a special alloy of silver, lead, sulphur, tin and copper, which is black in colour and used to fill

22

a pattern engraved on metal. There are many different ways of preparing the alloy, and they determine the strength and shade which ranges from a light grey to a velvety black. It is hard to say when niello work first appeared. It was known to the jewellers of Ancient Egypt, Greece, Rome and Byzantium. It was also found in Germany from the 8th century and in Italy from the 11th. But nowhere was the use of niello so long, widespread and various as in Russia. The jewellers of Old Russia

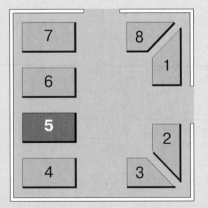

□ **22. Dish.**
*Moscow Kremlin
Workshops, 1561.
Gold; forging,
chasing, niello.
Diameter 42.3.
Belonged to Tsa-
rina Maria Temry-
ukovna*
□ **23. Censer.**
*Moscow Kremlin
Workshops, 1598.
Gold, gems;
chasing, niello.
Height 25, width
of wall 10.2.
Donated by Tsari-
na Irina Godunova
to the Archangel
Cathedral of the
Moscow Kremlin*

23

re familiar with niello in the 10th
tury. The real flowering of the art of
llo began in the middle of the 16th
tury, however.

e Armoury has some unique speci-
ns of niello work from the 16th to
h centuries. The niello graphics of
late 16th century are particularly
. An example is the round gold dish
ich was a wedding present from Ivan
Terrible to his second wife, the
bardinian Princess Maria Temriuk-
a, as can be seen from the inscrip-

tion round the edge. Dishes played an
important role in wedding rites in Old
Russia: they were used to bring the
bride her *kika* (headdress) and the
whole wedding attire and also to serve
special wedding food. After her death
the dish was sent to the Trinity Monastery of St Sergius in remembrance of
her. It is extremely simple in form and
refined in workmanship. Along the
edge is a band of fine velvety niello.
The form of the dish and ornament
were so perfect that subsequent gener-

24

□ **24. Small reliquary.** *Moscow Kremlin Workshops, 1589. Gold, gems, pearls; chasing, niello, casting. Height with top 11.8, width 6.5*

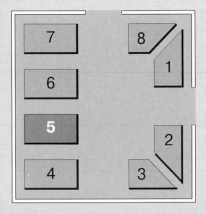

ations of Moscow masters, right up to the end of the 17th century, repeated the same motif of curved, flat lobes on a round plate and a smooth rim decorated with niello ornament and an inscription.

Another fine example of niello work is the gold censer in the form of a single-domed church presented by Irina Godunova, the wife of Tsar Theodore, to the Archangel Cathedral in the Moscow Kremlin, where the Moscow princes and tsars had been buried ever since the time of Prince Ivan Kalita.

□ **25. Chalice.**
Moscow, 1598.
Gold, gems;
chasing, niello,
carving. Height
27, diameter of
bowl 14.
Donated by Tsari-
na Irina Godunova
to the Archangel
Cathedral of the
Moscow Kremlin

25

lower section of the censer is dec-
ed with niello figures of saints. The
res are so light and natural that
seem to have been drawn with pen
paper rather than carved in metal.
unique quality of this work was ap-
iated by people of the day as well.
he beginning of the 17th century a
ial patriarchal decree was issued
ng that the censer should only be
nine times a year, on important
rch feasts.
small reliquary of 1589 is notewor-
for its elegance and fine niello pat-

tern. It consists of two panels with a
head-piece and is decorated with velvety niello and precious stones in high,
chased frames with pearls. At the side
of the lower panel is a carved inscription which says that the reliquary was
commissioned by Tsar Theodore for
his wife Irina. At the same time as the
censer and reliquary, Irina Godunova
also donated to the Archangel Cathedral a gold chalice of 1598 decorated
with a niello pattern and precious
stones.

Showcase 6

THE ART OF THE MOSCOW GOLDSMITHS IN THE 16TH CENTUR

The technique of enamelling became highly developed in the 16th century. As a rule the masters used enamel to fill in filigree patterns. There was a preference for elegant greyish-blue shades which combined well with large uncut stones, such as dark blue sapphires and pink tourmalines.

An example of this technique is the cover for the measuring icon of 1554 which belonged to Ivan the Terrible's son Ivan. It was so called because when Ivan was born an icon was made the same height as he was depicting the saint in whose honour he was christened. The cover is adorned with very fine filigree in the form of leaves and flowers intertwined with ribbons and covered with white, pale blue, green and dark blue enamel with seeds of gold, gems and pearls.

The art of the Moscow jewellers is clearly demonstrated by the cover of the 1571 Gospel donated by Ivan the Terrible to the Annunication Cathedral of the Moscow Kremlin. (By this time

26

□ **26. Gospel.** *Moscow Kremlin Workshops, 1571. Gold, gems, pearls; chasing, enamel, filigree, niello, seeds of gold. Height 42.5, width 30. Donated by Tsar Ivan the Terrible to the Annunciation Cathedral of the Moscow Kremlin*

□ **27. Measuring icon of St John Climacus.** *Moscow Kremlin Workshops, 1554. Gold, gems, pearls, wood; chasing, filigree, enamel, tempera. Height 46, width 17.2*

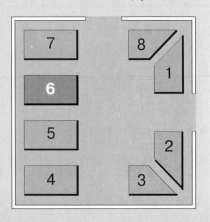

e had lost two wives and was prepar-
ng to take a third one. Ivan hoped that
y presenting the Gospel to the Annu-
ıcation Cathedral he might have a
appy marriage). Here too we find
hasing, in the five relief medallions,
iello work, in the inscriptions round
hese medallions, and enamelling in
ne fine gold lace. The colour of the
namel matches the colour of the pre-
ious stones adorning the cover. These
nclude a blue sapphire, Ivan the Terri-
le's favourite stone (the tsar thought
ne stone could help to "detect" trea-
on and drive away bad dreams).

ˉ this Gospel cover were the only ob-
ct to have survived, we would still be
ıstified in saying that the 16th century
ıarked the height of jewellery-making
ı Russia.

ˉot far from Ivan the Terrible's Gospel
ˉe three splendid panagia-cameos
ɑrved on three-layered sardonyx and
ɛpicting John the Baptist, Our Lady
f the Great Panagia and St John Cli-
ıacus. Specialists believe that the
ːones, which are similar in shape and
ɔlour, came from Venice. The choice
f saints (John the Baptist was the pa-
ˉon saint of Ivan the Terrible and John
ˉlimacus of his son Ivan), the style
ınd the iconography suggest that the
ɑrving on the cameo was done in
ˉoscow in the 16th century.

he panagias had gold mounts, but
ınly one of these has survived. The
ˉher two panagias were stolen in 1918
ˉom the Patriarchal vestry and, after
ɑssing through many hands and trav-
lling round the world, eventually re-
ırned to the Armoury fifty years later,
ınfortunately without their gold
ˉounts.

he 1560 icon of the Virgin Hodege-
ıa is an interesting specimen of 16th-
ɛntury jewellery. The elegant filigree
ˉnament on the case is covered with
ɛlicate enamel, precious stones and
ɛarls. The making of the case is con-
ɛcted with the family of Ivan the Ter-

27

28

□ **28. *Folding icon of St Nicholas the Miracle-Worker.*** *Moscow, 16th century. Gold, silver, gems, pearls; chasing, niello, carving, egg tempera. Length 24, width 15.5*

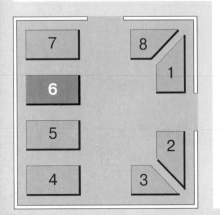

29

**29. *Panagia
with cameo in
mount.*** Moscow
Kremlin Work-
shops, mid-16th
century. Gold, sil-
ver, sardonyx,
gems, pearls;
casing, filigree,
enamel, carving,
niello. Height 16,
width 12

**30. *Cover for
Hodegetria
icon.*** Moscow,
16th century.
gold, gems; fili-
gree, enamel.
Height 47.5, width
38.5

30

ble, which explains the figures of patron saints of members of the royal family in the margins.

In the middle of the showcase on the right is a folding icon of St Nicholas the Miracle-Worker. The icon itself is silver, but its cover is gold decorated with gems and pearls. The intricate foliate pattern of the high-relief chasing is executed with a clear, precise symmetry. The icon was presented by Alexandra Bogdanovna Saburova, the wife of Ivan the Terrible's son, Ivan, to the Convent of the Intercession in Suzdal. At the "tsar's behest" Alexandra was imprisoned there shortly after her marriage under the name of the nun Yevdokia.

| Showcase 7 | NOVGOROD SILVERWARE OF THE 16TH TO 17TH CENTURIES |

After Novgorod became part of the Moscow state in 1478 the production of silverware expanded in the town. The work of the Moscow gold- and silversmiths influenced the produce of local silversmiths. A favourite technique was filigree, used to embellish icons, gospels, crosses and other objects. The craftsmen made the pattern out of three pieces of wire: a twisted piece in the middle and a smooth piece on either side. The pattern was often heart-shaped and then decorated with coloured enamel.

A fine example of Novgorodian filigree of the mid-16th century is the silver New Testament cover adorned with a dense ornament of scrolls and stems. It is also decorated with gems, cast figures of the four Evangelists and the Crucifixion in the middle. The background around the figures of the saints is enamelled in dark blue, black and green.

Novgorodian enamelwork of the 16th century is inferior to that of Moscow and has a somewhat restrained colour range, as can be seen from the 16th-century chalice from the St George Monastery in Novgorod. Along the rim of the smooth semi-spherical cup is an inscription on dark-blue enamel. The background has been chiselled out so that the words stand out in high relief. This technique is known as *obron*. Lower down, on a background of light green enamel is a carved Deisis, and lower still the figures of the Apostles Peter and Paul executed in lines filled with black enamel. The base of the chalice is older. It is thought to have been made in France in the 14th century.

Engraving on silver was not so popular with the Novgorodian masters as filigree or enamel work. This is not to say that Novgorod lacked skilled silver engravers, however. The Armoury, the History Museum and the Russian Museum have six drinking vessels of exquisite workmanship made by the Novgorodian craftsman Grigory Ivanov, who was nicknamed Novgorodets. He had lost his legs, and it was physically difficult for him to create whole objects, so he limited himself to embellishing finished articles with fine carving.

The beakers exhibited in this showcase were made for Metropolitan Pitirim of Novgorod, who was later the patriarch of all Russia. The smooth surface is decorated with gilded carving reminiscent of a carpet. The fine ornament of ribbons, stylised foliate scrolls and large flowers is dotted with heads of

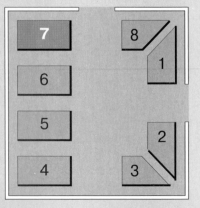

31

□ **31. Gospel.** *Russia, Novgorod, 16th century. Silver, gems, glass, paper; filigree, enamel, casting, carving, chasing, gilding. Height 36.5, width 23*

cherubim, birds and fish (in the 17th century a swimming fish was a symbol of hope, peace, security and ecclesiastical peace). The drawings on the beakers testify to the craftsman's rich imagination and also his extensive knowledge of engravings and book illustrations and the language of mediaeval mysticism.

The Novgorodian silversmiths greatly influenced the development of applied art in many Russian artistic centres, Moscow included. Their techniques and ornament can often be found in articles produced in the Gold and Silver Chambers of the Moscow Kremlin.

32

□ **32. Beaker.** Russia, Novgorod, 1670s. Master G.Ivanov. Silver; carving, gilding. Height 24.6, diameter 13.4.
Belonged to Patriarch Pitirim

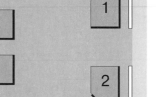

□ **33. Chalice.** *Bowl – Russia, Novgorod, early 16th century. Stand – France (?), 14th century. Silver; casting, enamel, carving, gilding. Height 23.9, diameter of cup 15.3*

Showcase 8	THE COVERS ON THE SHRINES OF TSAREVICH DMITRI AND ST CYRIL OF BELOZERSK

Since 1987 the Armoury has exhibited two rare specimens of exquisite sculptural chasing from the first half of the 17th century, the cover from the shrine (1630) of Tsarevich Dmitri in the Archangel Cathedral of the Moscow Kremlin and the cover from the shrine (1643) of St Cyril of Belozersk, which were both made in the Silver Chamber of the Moscow Kremlin. The work was supervised by one of the finest jewellers of the day, Gavriil Ovdokimov, "chartered master of the first class".

Three such unique items of decorative applied art have survived in Russia: two in the Armoury and one in the Russian Museum. The third is the cover for the shrine of St Alexander of Svir, a donation by Tsar Michael Romanov to the St Alexander of Svir Monastery near the town of Olonets, from which it came to the Russian Museum in 1923. Specialists believe that the shrine of Alexander of Svir could have been made by the same group of silversmiths under Gavrila Ovdokimov.

All three specimens are splendid examples of sculptural chasing and have a similar composition, realistic treatment of the face, arrangement of figures in a background densely covered with foliate ornament, and excellent chasing.

The silver shrine of Tsarevich Dmitri who died in tragic circumstances at the end of the 16th century was commissioned by Tsar Michael. All that remains of it is the cover. The shrine itself was stolen during the war of 1812.

The cover from the shrine of Cyril of Belozersk, the founder of the monastery and great churchman of the 14th century, was thought to be lost. And only thanks to the specialist at the museum preserve E.V.Shakurova and the talented restorers V.M.Germanyuk, N.A.Dolgov and A.B.Naumov has it been possible to recreate this work, of which about thirty fragments survived in different museums. The fragments were repaired, washed and fastened to a wooden frame. A careful study of them and the subsequent restoration of the cover suggested that it had belonged to St Cyril of Belozersk, which was borne out by the inscription on two fragments: "the Venerable Cyril", "Miracle-worker of Belozersk", and also the texts of his vita.

In view of the exceptional importance of the inscription for an historical description of the item we shall quote it in full: "In the reign of His Majesty the Tsar and Grand Prince Mikhail Fyo-

□ **34. Shrine of St Cyril of Belozersk (cover).** *Moscow Kremlin Workshops, 1643. Silver; chasing, casting, gilding. Length 196, width 72*

dorovich of all Russia and his God-fearing and Christ-loving Tsarina and Grand Princess Evdokia and their noble offspring the God-fearing Tsarevich Prince Oleksei Mikhailovich and the Tsarevna Princess Anna Mikhailovna and the God-fearing Princess Tatiana Mikhailovna, and the Most Holy Iosif, Patriarch of Moscow and All Russia, this shrine for the Venerable Miracle-Worker Kiril Beloozersky was commissioned by Fyodor Ivanovich Sheremetiev in the time of Higumen Antonii and the Cellarer elder Savatii Yushkov in the year 7151." (i.e., 1642 or 1643).

Research in the archives and on all the inscriptions on the fragments has made it possible to reconstruct the history of the Venerable Cyril's shrine. It was commissioned in 1643 by the boyar Fyodor Ivanovich Sheremetiev, an eminent statesman in the reign of Tsar Michael, who was in charge of the Armoury, the Great Treasury and the silversmiths, and installed in the monastery at Kirillov, where the boyar's parents, wife and only son were buried and where he himself took monastic vows in 1645 under the name of Theodosius and was buried in the front porch of the Assumption Cathedral. The most important of Sheremetiev's rich donations to the St Cyril of Beloz-

ersk Monastery is the shrine for its founder, St Cyril, which became the monastery's most treasured possession..

The chased figures of St Cyril of Belozersk and Tsarevich Dmitri are remarkably expressive and convey some individual features. They are portrayed full-length: Dmitri in royal robes and Cyril in the dress of a schema monk, holding an unrolled scroll in one hand, with the other raised in blessing. The scroll is chased with an inscription in elaborate ligatured script. Their faces retain some lively features – the open eyes, dimpled cheek and chubbiness of young Dmitri, and Cyril's wrinkled forehead, hollow cheeks, stern expression under the arched brows and firmly pressed lips. His face conveys a state of spiritual concentration, ascetic immobility and at the same time intense inspiration.

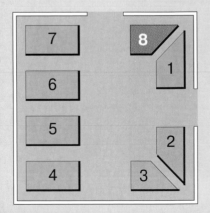

35. Shrine of
?revich Dmitri
?ver). *Moscow*
?mlin Work-
?ps, 1630. Sil-
?gems; chas-
?casting, gild-
?Length 157,
?h 70

ROOM 2

RUSSIAN GOLD AND SILVERWARE OF THE 17TH TO EARLY 20TH CENTURIES

Showcase 9

MOSCOW JEWELLERY – FIRST HALF OF 17TH CENTURY

The Polish-Lithuanian intervention at the beginning of the 17th century devastated the state coffers. The rebirth of the state began after the enemy were driven out in 1612.

The Armoury possesses the fullest and most varied collection of articles made by Russian craftsmen at the beginning of the 17th century. They were all produced in the workshops of the Moscow Kremlin – the Armoury, Stables Office, Tsarina's, Gold and Silver chambers. The masters of the early 17th century continued to work in the traditions of the preceding century.

The gold censer in the lefthand section of the showcase was made in 1616 by Danila Osipov and Tretyak Pestrikov. In form and arrangement of precious stones it reminds one of Irina Goduno-

36

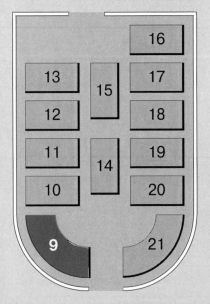

va's censer, which you saw in case 5, but instead of the fine niello ornament it is decorated with chasing. Around the base is a niello inscription in ornamental ligatured script to the effect that the censer was a gift by Tsar Michael to the Trinity Monastery of St Sergius.

The gold cover for the 1631–1632 Gospel exhibited here was the work of

6. *Censer.*
cow, 1616.
ters in the Sil-
Chamber:
sipov and
estrikov. Gold;
sing, niello.
ht with cross
, width of
e 11

7. *Gospel.*
cow, first half
7th century.
ter:
vdokimov,
2. Gold,
s, pearls;
sing, enamel.
ht 42.5, width

ated by Tsar
ael Romanov
e Trinity
astery
Sergius

37

vrila Ovdokimov, the same master, may remember, who fashioned the nes of St Cyril of Belozersk and ace Dmitri. He worked in the Silver mber of the Moscow Kremlin for re than forty years. Ovdokimov re-ted the composition of the 1571 er (see case 6), but here new ten-cies have clearly made themselves , namely, the love of patterns and ornament in general. The precious stones and enamelling are much brighter. Moreover, there is coloured enamel not only on the filigree orna-ment but also on the architectural de-tails. The Gospel was made as a gift for the Trinity Monastery of St Sergius. The gold cover for the icon of Our Lady of Tenderness (first third of 17th cent.) is decorated with brightly col-

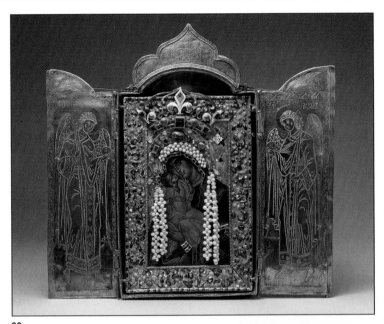

38

□ **38.** *Cover for icon of Our Lady of Tenderness.* Moscow, first third of 17th century. Gold, gems, pearls; filigree, enamel. Height 22, width 14.8

39

☐ **39. Gospel.** *Moscow, 1613. Silver, gems, pearls, velvet, paper; chasing, niello, gilding. Height 45, width 28.5. Belonged to Prince Dmitry Pozharsky*

☐ **40. Cover for icon of the Trinity.** *Russia, late 16th – early 17th century. Silver; gilding, chasing, carving, niello. Height 154, width 130. Donated by D.I.Godunov to the Ipatievsky Monastery in Kostroma*

40

red enamel, as is the small but elegant loving-cup of Yevdokia Lukyavna (Tsar Michael's wife) with its conical top.

e gilded silver cover of the manuript Gospel of 1613, decorated with ello work and large semi-precious nes with pearls, is executed in the le of 16th-century decorative and plied art. The Gospel belonged to ince Dmitry Pozharsky and this preus cover was ordered by him.

the middle of the showcase is a gold er for the icon of the Trinity (late 16th – early 17th cent.), a gift from the boyar Dmitri Ivanovich Godunov (Tsar Boris's uncle) to the Ipatievsky Monastery in Kostroma. The precise rhythm of the chased pattern and the stones in their high frames are most effective.

Showcase 10

RUSSIAN TABLEWARE OF THE 17TH CENTURY

Mediaeval Russia was famed for its tableware. The dippers, loving-cups, goblets, wine-bowls and beakers, all the everyday utensils displayed in this showcase, give a fairly clear idea of the variety of forms and features.

Naturally only people of high birth had gold and silver tableware adorned with precious stones and pearls. The utensils used by the common people had just the same form, however, although they were made of less "noble" materials, wood and clay.

Note the so-called "boat-shaped" dippers. This is a purely Russian form which goes back to the dim and distant past. Dippers first appeared in the North with its many rivers and lakes abounding in wild duck, geese and swans, where the people built wooden

boats in the form of water fowl and where, way back in the second millenium B.C., they made small oval wooden dippers. Later they began to produce gold and silver dippers modelled on the wooden ones. Depending on what they were used for they had different names, such as "guest", "home", "presentation", "burial", and "mead" dippers. People drank mead from them. The colour of the mead determined the choice of dipper. Red mead was served in gold dippers, white mead in silver dippers and foreign wine in goblets.

Of special interest in this case are three dippers which belonged to Tsar Michael. Each of them was made from a single nugget of gold and weighs from one-and-a-half to two kilograms. Such dippers were rarely used for drinking, usually only on special feast days. The rest of the time they stood on special shelves as symbols of the richness of the tsar's court.

Dippers were often used as rewards for military valour, ambassadorial service, tax-collection, or loyal service by Cossack leaders and elders. The base was decorated with a two-headed eagle and an inscription, which contained the name of the person to whom it had been awarded and the service he had performed.

Another widespread form of drinking vessel was the loving-cup — a large bowl which was passed from hand to hand for each guest to drink from in turn. Here you can see the various types of loving-cups used in Russia. At

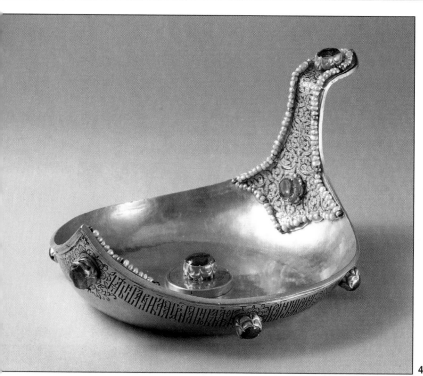

41

□ **41. Dipper.**
*Moscow Kremlin
Workshops, 1618.
Gold, gems,
pearls; forging,
niello. Height 15,
length 30, width
22.
Belonged to Tsar
Michael Romanov*

□ **42. Quaiches.** *Moscow, 17th century. Cornelian, mountain crystal, agate, gold; enamel, niello. Height 4.0, diameter 6.5, width with handle 9.7.*

*Height 3.4, diameter 6.1, width with handle 8.2.
Height 2.6, diameter 4.2, width with handle 5.8.*

first glance they may all look the same, but this is not the case. The main thing about a loving-cup is not its shape, but the ornament and inscription round the rim. The latter usually includes the name of the owner, with some kind of utterance or exhortation.

The loving-cup presented to Tsar Michael in 1618 by the wife of the Duma secretary Pyotr Tretyakov with a request to pardon her husband who had been charged with treason is a fine work of art. The cup is decorated with high-relief chased ornament and is supported by six human figures. Engraved round the rim is the following inscription: "True love is like a gold vessel, nothing can break it, and should it get slightly bent, good sense will soon put it right."

Note the small gold loving-cup presented to Tsar Michael Romanov who in turn presented it to his second wife Yevdokia, which is why the donators' niello inscription in circles was removed at his request and pearling was added to the ornament. A vessel such as this could have been used as a cup

43

44

□ **44. Loving-cup.** *Moscow Kremlin Workshops, first half of 17th century. Gold, gems, pearls; niello. Height 15, diameter of rim 9.3*

45

43. Loving-cup. *Moscow, first quarter of 17th century. Silver; chasing, casting, carving, gilding. Height with lid 28.5, diameter of rim 14.4*

☐ **45. Endova bowl.** *Moscow, 1644. Silver; chasing, carving, gilding. Height 17, diameter 30. Belonged to the high-ranking boyar V.I.Streshnev*

...ced on the grave of some dear de-...rted person and filled with honey-...eetened water.

...ere was widespread use of *korchiki* ...nall dippers on bases) and goblets ...de of agate, cornelian and moun-...n crystal. Strong drinks and mead ...re served in them. Many have pre-...ved the names of their owners.

...the back of the case is a chased sil-...bowl (*endova*) which belonged to

Vassily Streshnev who was in charge of the offices of gold- and silver-work in the Armoury from 1630 to 1635. This round bowl with a lip at the top was probably used as a vessel for holding drink. It was made in 1644 and is a rare specimen of its kind.

Showcase 11

NIELLO AND CARVING – SECOND HALF OF 17TH CENTURY

In the second half of 17th century Russian craftsmen improved the technique not only of enamelling, but also of carving and niello work. At the beginning of the century niello masters had mostly continued and developed the devices and ornament of the preceding century.

In the middle of the 17th century Greek jewellers from Constantinople came to Moscow and greatly influenced the development of niello work in Russia. In 1662 the Greeks Konstantin Manuilov and Filipp Pavlov petitioned the Russian tsar for permission to live in Moscow for a year or two, open a workshop and show the Muscovites their art of working gold with niello. And should their works be to the liking of the tsar, they were ready to take apprentices and teach them the secrets of their craft. The masters from Constantinople received permission and their works were popular with the Moscow nobility. True, we know nothing of their "teaching activity".

More detailed information has survived on two other jewellers from Constantinople – Ivan Yuriev and Leonty Konstantinov, who spent more than three years in Moscow from 1664 to 1667. They really did teach the art of niello to several Moscow craftsmen.

In the second half of the 17th century the nature of niello decoration changed. Soft niello ornament became a background for a large gilded pattern of grasses, flowers on long stems, garlands of fruit, sweet-william and fans. The influence of the Orient is felt in particular in the ornament of the flat round plate here which belonged to Prince V.V.Golitsyn.

The silver plate which belonged to the head of the Armoury Office and the Gold and Silver Chambers, the boyar Bogdan Matveyevich Khitrovo, is highly original in form and decoration. Along the broad edge of the plate are carved wavy strips of gilt and niello with an ornament of flowers and leaves and in the middle is the Khitrovo coat-of-arms – a hand holding a sword crossed by two sabres.

The foliate ornament of the late 17th century is more realistic than that of the 16th. This is well illustrated by the elegant silver cutlery stand with a pointed top made by the Russian jewellers Mikhail Mikhailovich and An-

46

☐ **46. Plate.**
Moscow, 1667–
1676. Silver;
niello, carving,
gilding. Diameter
30.2.
Belonged to
the boyar
B.M.Khitrovo
☐ **47. Plate.**
Moscow, end
of 17th century.
Silver; niello,
carving, gilding.
Diameter 26.9

48

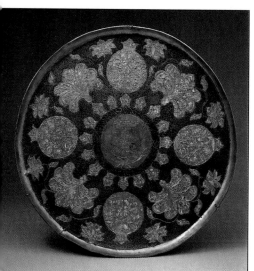

☐ **48. Cutlery stand.** Moscow Kremlin Work-
shops, 1685. Silver; niello, carving, gilding.
Height 12.2, diameter 12.2.
Belonged to Tsarevna Sophia Alexeyevna

☐ **49. Cutlery stand.** *Moscow, end of 17th century. Silver; niello, carving, gilding. Diameter 14.6, height 10.*
Belonged to Tsar Peter the Great
☐ **50. Beaker.** *Moscow Kremlin Workshops, end of 17th century. Master: V.Andreyev. Silver; chasing, carving, gilding. Height 21, diameter of rim 13.7*

49   50

drei Pavlov (1685) and Peter the Great's silver cutlery stand decorated with niello.

The technique of carving on metal was flat and linear until the last third of the 17th century, depicting grasses, people and animals in outline only, without shading. At the end of the 17th century more complicated subjects were borrowed from book illustrations and engravings. The engraver Vassily Andreyev, who worked at the Patriarchal Court in Moscow, attained great mastery in metal carving. His works have depth, perspective and dynamism. Andreyev embellished goblets, mugs and other vessels with free, light carving, skilfully alternating a silver and a gilt pattern. He took many subjects from

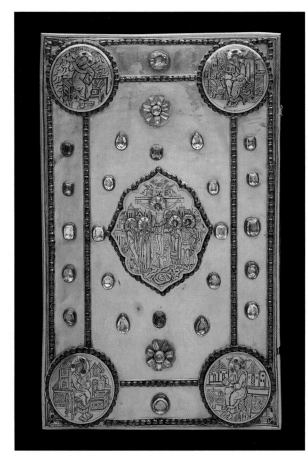

□ **51. Gospel.**
Moscow, 1668.
Gold, silver,
gems; niello,
carving, chasing.
Length 49, width
30.5.
Donated by Tsar
Alexis to the Chu-
dov Monastery in
the Moscow
Kremlin

51

Bible and made use of the patterns
Simon Ushakov, an outstanding
ssian artist of the late 17th century,
ose work marked the transition from
diaeval icon-painting to secular
ist art. The tall silver beaker with
ved, multi-figured compositions
the small silver beaker on ball-
ped legs are two of his finest works.
u are bound to notice the gold Gos-
cover decorated with amethysts
rubies. The special way in which
metal has been forged gives its

gilded surface an unusual matt effect.
The Gospel was a gift by Tsar Alexis
and his family to the Chudov Monastery.

Showcase 12   RUSSIAN COLOURED ENAMEL

The items in this case are unusually bright and colourful. The caskets, bowls, cups, rouge boxes, knives, forks and religious objects all have the form typical of 17th-century silverware. The main thing here, however, is not the form, but the enamel ornament and the choice of colours. Bright yellow sunflowers, blue cornflowers, pinkish-mauve tulips with black veins, daisies combined with emerald green and a pure white background – this dazzling play of colours is the work of the famous Solvychegodsk masters.

At the end of the 17th century the Solvychegodsk silversmiths were the first to execute painting on enamel. The technique consisted of applying a layer of enamel in one shade only to the object, fusing it by heating, then

52

53

☐ **52. Bowl.** *Russia, Solvychegodsk, late 17th century. Silver; enamel. Height 5.4, diameter 15.2*
☐ **53. Casket.** *Russia, Solvychegodsk, late 17th century. Silver, enamel. Height 11, base length 19.5, base width 11*

□ **54. Bowl.**
Russia, Solvyche-
godsk, late 17th
century. Silver;
enamel. Height
4.7, diameter
15.8

54

lying a pattern in special paints
n volatile oils and fusing it again.
·y were skilled at enamelling spher-
objects without any previous out-
ng and had a special technique of
·forcing the pattern with filigree
·. The Solvychegodsk enamellers
not limit themselves to the flower
·ament which dominates in their
·k. In their articles we also find ani-
·s, birds, complex compositions on
·ical themes, subjects from Western
·ravings, book illustrations and
·es from everyday life. Note the
·s with subjects from the Bible story
·ut Samson and allegorical scenes
·the theme of the five senses: taste,
·ll, hearing, sight and touch. Al-
·ugh the portrayal of the human face
· figure is still somewhat primitive,
·se are the first attempts to create
· miniature portraits on enamel
·ch became so widespread in the
·h century.

The art of the Solvychegodsk jewellers
influenced the enamelwork of many
Russian towns, such as Veliky Ustyug,
Vyatka, Yaroslavl and Moscow.

Showcase 13

17TH-CENTURY SILVERWARE FROM THE CITIES ON THE VOLGA

Here you will find a collection of 17th-century articles from artistic centres on the Volga. The Volga area is one of dense forests, and from very early times was a centre of woodcarving. This art was handed down from generation to generation. The ornamental motifs of woodcarving became reflected in the patterns used by the silversmiths.

The most important centre of the Volga area was Yaroslavl. The city was exceptionally well located for trading. English, Dutch and German merchants hastened to open up trading offices there. All this promoted the widespread development of arts and crafts in the town, such as wood-carving, printing on textiles, tile-making, metal- and silver-work.

55

The articles produced by the Yaroslavl silversmiths show a remarkable richness of form and ornament and a high level of technical skill. The Yaroslavl craftsmen mastered to perfection such a complex technique as high-relief chasing, for example. The large flowers, curving stems, fruit and foliage, and figures of animals and people are woven together into a single pattern which covers the whole object. In all

s one can sense the traditions of
odcarving.

ical specimens of Yaroslavl metal
sing are the silver censer and thuri-
from the Church of St Nicholas the
t, displayed in the case. The crafts-
n succeeded in combining brilliant-
two quite different techniques, high-
ief chasing and light contour carv-
. The 1697 diskos (a church plate
h a base) is also executed in this
y.

e chalices made in Yaroslavl in 1697
displayed here have an unusual
line. The small cup is attached to a
pyramidal stand. The floral orna-
nt on the stand emphasises the py-
nidal form.

e silversmiths of Yaroslavl were
ed for their skill and invited to the
rkshops of the Moscow Kremlin
the Trinity Monastery of St Ser-
s. In the 17th century, for example,
Yaroslavians Mikhail Grigoriev,
nyon Vassiliev and Sergei Yaro-
vets worked on the iconostasis of the
sumption Cathedral in the Moscow
emlin.

other important artistic centre on
Volga was Kostroma. Kostroma sil-
ware has much in common with lo-
decorative woodcarving. It is em-
ished with low-relief chasing and
dense foliate ornament. The
sed pattern is sometimes replaced
flat, carefully worked casting.
e two silver censers dated 1641 and
76 respectively are from the Epipha-
Monastery in Kostroma. They have
interesting and unusual shape. The
per section is in the form of a high
t-like roof decorated with open-
rk cast ornament of foliate braiding.
e alternating gold and silver sections
ke them look light and elegant.
e silver chalice of 1685 is a fine ex-
ple of Nizhny Novgorod workman-
p. The large silver cup is adorned
h rich chased ornament and the
nbols of the Evangelists. The chal-

56

☐ **55. Chalice.** Russia, Yaroslavl, 1697.
Silver; chasing, carving, gilding. Height 28.7,
diameter of cup 16.3
☐ **56. Censer.** Russia, Kostroma, 17th
century. Silver, cornelian; casting, chasing,
carving, gilding. Height 40, diameter of cup
12

ice was a gift from Archimandrite Sergius to the Makariev Zheltovodsky
Trinity Monastery.

Showcase 14

MOSCOW ENAMELWORK – SECOND HALF OF 17TH CENTURY

The strengthening of centralised power after the defeat of the Polish-Lithuanian and Swedish armies at the beginning of the 17th century, a successful foreign policy and the joining of the Ukraine to Russia all had a beneficial effect on the development of the arts. The main features of artistic style during this period are vigour, brilliance and colour. Objects were adorned with green emeralds, blue sapphires, red rubies, mauve amethysts and shining enamel so rich and radiant that it even rivals the precious stones.

A fine example of this is the enamel on the gold loving-cup displayed here. The craftsman gave the cup the shape of a half-open flower and showed great taste in his choice of colours, which remind one of a blossoming spring meadow. Around the rim in black enamel is an inscription to the effect that the cup was a gift from Patriarch Nikon to Tsar Alexis in 1653. There is another inscription which says that the cup was presented to Prince V.V.Golitsyn in 1686 for his services in connection with the conclusion of a lasting peace with Poland. Three years later the prince found himself in disgrace, however. His possessions were confiscated and handed over to the royal treasury, including this enamelled gold cup.

The huge gold chalice presented by the boyar's wife A.I.Morozova to the Chudov Monastery in the Moscow Kremlin in 1664 is a masterpiece of 17th-century enamelwork. The cup is embellished with bright enamelled foliate ornament framing oval medallions with figures from the Deisis, and also emeralds, sapphires, rubies and diamonds in gold mounts. The chalice's stand and base are adorned with exquisite white and blue enamel.

On all the objects of this period the casting and chasing is beautifully combined with enamel. Whereas in the 16th century an article was made by a single craftsman who did all the types of work, in the 17th the masters in the Gold and Silver chambers began to specialise. Thus, the gold cover of the 1678 Gospel on display was the work of Mikhail Vassiliev, Dmitri Terentiev and the enameller Frobos. The cover was commissioned by Tsar Theodore, son of Alexis, for the Kremlin palace church of Our Saviour Not

□ **57. Bowl.** *Moscow Kremlin Workshops, 1653.*
Gold, gems; enamel. Height 8.4, diameter 15.
Gift from Patriarch Nikon to Tsar Alexis

57

Made By Hands (the Upper Saviour
Cathedral).

This Gospel is of interest not only because of its fine cover. If you open it,
you will find no less than 1,200 illumi-
nated miniatures by seven Russian artists under the supervision of the well-
known Moscow icon-painter Fyodor
Zubov.

The striving of jewellers in the second
half of the 17th century for greater ornament and sumptuousness occasionally resulted in objects being overload-
ed with gems, pearls and enamel. In
1657 the goldsmith Pyotr Ivanov was
commissioned by Patriarch Nikon to
make the gold cover displayed here for
the icon of Our Lady of Vladimir. Note
the two huge emeralds, each weighing

. Chalice. *Moscow Kremlin Workshops,*
Gold, gems; enamel. Height 26, diameter
o 16.5.
ted by the boyar's wife A.I.Morozova to the
ov Monastery in the Moscow Kremlin

59

☐ **59. Gospel.** *Moscow Kremlin Workshops, 1678. Gold, gems, paper; chasing, enamel. Height 47, width 29.6.*
Donated by Tsar Theodore to the Upper Saviour Cathedral in the Moscow Kremlin

carats, the equivalent of 20 grams. n emeralds are found only rarely in re. During this period large num- of gems were purchased in India China, and occasionally in West- Europe. Pearls and mother-of- l came from Russian rivers.
ards the end of the 17th century e was a tendency to create more est objects. The exhibits include a Gospel commissioned by Tsar odore, son of Alexis (on the other of the case). The only ornament on the smooth gilded surface of the cover are five enamelled plates framed with flat rubies. Although this refined austerity testifies to the jeweller's good taste, it was not widely acknowledged by 17th-century craftsmen. The articles produced in this period are remarkable for their sumptuous ornament.

On the other side of the showcase are specimens of Moscow silver. By comparison with the bright colourful enamel on gold made by Kremlin mas-

☐ **60. Plate.**
Moscow Kremlin Workshops, 1675. Gold; enamel. Diameter 22.2. Belonged to Tsar Alexis

60

ters in the second half of the 17th century, the items here seem far more modest.

These articles were also fashioned by Moscow craftsmen and also belong to the second half of the 17th century. However, as you can see, the enamel is applied not to gold, but to silver filigree ornament. Hence too the restrained colour shades: whites, greens and pale blues, because silver has a lower melting point. The appearance of these articles is explained largely by the growth of the urban population's demand for artistically made household objects. The Moscow craftsmen in the so-called Silver Row filled the city's markets with all manner of tableware, goblets, beakers and spoons, all sorts of cosmetic boxes for eye-

61

☐ **61. *Cover for icon of Our Lady of Vladimir.***
*Moscow, 1657. Master: P.Ivanov. Gold, gems;
chasing. Length 105, width 70*

brow make-up and rouge, icon covers and sections of them, such as haloes and hanging crescents. Silver rings and earrings with cheap stones and coloured glass were very widespread, as were enamelled crosses which were worn on broad, flat chains. All these articles, made for the most part of low-grade silver, formed part of the dowry not only of wealthy sections of the urban population, but also of the peasantry. A favourite decoration with craftsmen was enamel in subdued shades on silver filigree ornament. From the 16th century this type of technique became widespread in all the artistic centres of the Russian state. **A** special role in Moscow articles of the 17th century was played by white enamel, which provided an excellent foil for the blues, greens and blacks and was sometimes the only colour. Jewellers often used enamel to fill filigree rings, thus forming little balls that looked like pearls or beads. Enamel "pearling" was a widespread device very popular with Russian craftsmen during this period.

□ **62. Loving-cup.** *Moscow, 1662. Masters V. and F. Ivanov. Ivory, silver, gems; chasing, filigree, gilding, enamel. Height 15.5, diameter 11.5*

62

The ivory loving-cup made in 1662 by the brothers Vassily and Fyodor Ivanov, who worked in the Silver Chamber, has a lovely enamel pattern. The silver mounting is adorned with enamel stems and white and blue beading. The radiance of the enamel contrasts with the matt surface of the ivory to good effect.

63

□ **63. Gospel.** *Moscow, 1681. Gold, gems; chasing, enamel. Height 41.5, width 28.5*

Showcase 15

JEWELLERY – FIRST HALF OF THE 18TH CENTURY

In the late 17th and early 18th centuries changes of great historical significance took place in Russia. The beginning of the 18th century in Russian history was marked by the state and economic reforms of Peter the Great. The tsar moved the capital from Moscow to St Petersburg. Because the vast expenditure on military needs and the building of the new capital required more and more gold and silver, Peter issued a decree restricting the use of these metals for domestic objects, which naturally led to a reduction in the making of jewellery. In 1711 many craftsmen were moved to St Petersburg to work in the newly founded Armoury Court which "specialised" in the manufacture of arms and various machines. On the tsar's orders some masters were

sent to Voronezh and Archangel to work in the shipyards there.

Nevertheless the art of jewellery-making continued to develop. The ornament on Russian gold and silverware, while retaining its national features, developed along the same lines as that on precious articles produced in Western Europe. The sumptuousness of 18th-century silverware is enhanced by enamel painting. Painting with enamel paints on an enamel background was known in the 17th century as well, but in the 18th it became most widespread. Plates of bright enamel are used to adorn gospel covers, chalices, medallions, orders and caskets. From the articles in this hall you can trace how Russian enamellers perfected their art, advancing from a profusion of colourful ornament to the refined portrait miniature and fine painting on elegant gold snuffboxes, clocks and panagias.

The work of the Russian enamel portrait painters A.Ovsov and G.Musikiisky (early 18th cent.) won worldwide fame. Both masters were employed in the Armoury and later moved to St Petersburg. Their articles can be found in museums in Moscow and Petersburg and in private collections abroad.

In the middle of this case is an oval gold snuffbox. The lid, which is decorated with smooth transparent reddish-brown enamel, bears a portrait of Peter the Great executed by A.Ovsov. This artist created a series of excellent miniature portraits. His work is characterised by pure, vivid colours and precise, clear drawing.

64

4. Insignia.
sia, early 17th
tury. Gold, sil-
diamonds;
mel. Height
, width 7.1

5. Snuffbox
s, 1712–
3. Miniature –
etersburg,
7. Enameller:
vsov. Gold,
per; enamel,
aving. Height
length 9.2,
15.2

65

Here too you can see a pectoral insignia of 1707 and panagia of 1720 with enamelled medallions by the well-known miniature portrait painter Grigory Musikiisky. His earliest work is the silver panagia with a miniature of Peter the Great taken from the portrait of 1697 by Kneller. The young Peter is portrayed wearing armour and a sable cloak in the traditions of the formal portrait of the first half of the 18th century. The enamel composition on the other panagia of the Virgin's Lament was executed in 1720 and bears the artist's signature.

During this period the portrait miniature became so popular that a special enamelwork class was introduced in the Russian Academy of Arts.

Russian silversmiths continued to develop the art of the filigree pattern. Openwork filigree ornament was not soldered on, but simply placed on a smooth gold or silver background.

Filigree played an important part in the jewellery-making of mediaeval Russia. The pattern, invariably calm, smooth and rhythmical, was primarily of a foliate nature.

At this time one does not find items in which filigree is the only type of decoration. As a rule, it is combined with plastic forms, chased and cast reliefs, for which it serves as a background. Filigree is inserted into the framing of such items as small ivory, wood or stone icons, crosses and panagias. In the 18th century one finds articles made entirely of open-work filigree ornament.

The masters managed to avoid making the filigree ornament look flat by adding linings of silver gilt, coloured glass or metal covered with coloured enamel.

The elegant soup bowl on a Petersburg dish of 1737 is executed in this technique. Here the silver filigree is applied to the smooth silver gilt surface of the bowl and dish.

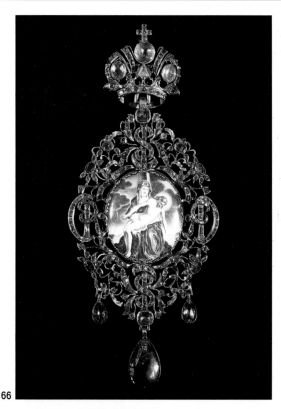

66

□ **66. *Panagia.***
*Miniature – St
Petersburg, 1720.
Enameller:
G.Musikiisky.
Mount – mid-18th
century. Silver,
gems; chasing,
enamel. Height
21, width 9.5*
□ **67. *Soup
bowl.*** *St Peters-
burg, 1737.
Silver; chasing,
filigree, gilding.
Height 7.4,
diameter 15.2*

67

Showcase 16

GOLD AND SILVERWARE FROM 1740 TO 1760. MOSCOW AND ST PETERSBURG

The economic changes, broader relations with Europe, growth of trade and the introduction of European standards led to the appearance of new types of tableware and clothing. Great changes took place in the everyday life of the Russian nobility. Instead of the traditional wooden buildings stone palaces were built in the new capital where splendid assemblies took place. The articles produced by Russian silversmiths during this period show a great variety and richness of form. New types of food and drink came into fashion, such as tea, coffee and cocoa, and this in turn required new utensils, namely, coffee- and teapots, milk-jugs, samovars and services. Traditional Russian drinking vessels were no longer used. Dippers and loving-cups lost

68

□ **68. Reliquary.** *Moscow, 1753. Silver; chasing, casting, gilding. Height 69.5, width 24.1*

69

☐ **69. Presentation dipper.** *Moscow, 1755. Silver; chasing, casting, gilding. Height 22.5, length 40.5, width 19.5*
☐ **70. Soup bowl.** *St Petersburg, 18th century. Gold, diamonds; chasing, carving. Height 32, diameter of tray 47*

70

their boat shape and turned into decorative vases, used as gifts and rewards for services.

Russian art experienced the influence of European rococo.

The main technique of rococo was metal casting and high-relief chasing. In the middle of the case you can see a typical example of this style, a reliquary made in Moscow in 1753. It has an intricate form and rich ornament which covers the surface entirely. The dynamic figures of Christ and the Evangelists are executed in the technique of casting.

A fine specimen of rococo by 18th-century Petersburg masters is the silver soup bowl on a stand displayed here. It is decorated with relief rocaille ornament (in the form of a scroll). The shells with the monogram "A" under a crown are supported, as it were, by the figures of two cast eagles. On the lid are rich cartouches of fruit and flowers garlands.

The snuffboxes of this period are worthy of attention. Note the large gold snuffbox studded with diamonds which was made for Empress Elizabeth, Peter the Great's daughter, in 1759 by one of the finest court jewellers and diamond workers of the period, Jérémie Pauzié who walked all the way to Russia in 1729 from Switzerland at the age of fifteen. For seven years he studied under the Petersburg jeweller Benedict Gravero, who worked at the court of Empress Anne. Pauzié gradually mastered the skills of his craft and won more and more commissions, to become one of the best known jewellers of his day. The lid of the snuffbox bears an applied profile portrait of Empress Elizabeth, remarkable for the beauty and fineness of the design. On the sides of the snuffbox are four allegorical scenes connected with events during the early years of Elizabeth's reign. The snuffbox itself belonged to the Razumovsky family.

Among the presentation plates a decorative plate by the Moscow craftsman Pyotr Afinogenov stands out in particular. In the centre is a scene from the Bible story of Esther, framed with rocaille ornament. Afinogenov borrowed the composition of the scene from an engraving from the Piscator Bible, which he adapted creatively to suit the technique of silver-working. The Armoury has twenty-one articles by this master.

71

72

□ **71. Dish.**
*Moscow, 1767.
Master:
P.Afinogenov.
Silver; chasing,
carving, casting,
gilding. Diameter
54*
□ **72. Snuff-
box.** *St Peters-
burg, mid-18th
century. Master:
J.Pauzié. Gold,
brilliants; chasing,
carving. Height
4.6, diameter 11*

Showcase 17

GOLD AND SILVERWARE FROM PROVINCIAL CENTRES – 18TH TO 19TH CENTURIES

In this showcase you will find articles by the craftsmen of Veliky Ustyug and Tobolsk.

Veliky Ustyug was the largest town on the trade route from Archangel to Moscow and also from Novgorod and Moscow to Siberia. There was a saying that "Nothing is ever done in Siberia without the Ustyugians". At the beginning of the 18th century the centre of trade, industry and culture in the north of Russia moved from Solvychegodsk to Veliky Ustyug. The technique of niello work became most highly developed in this town. Veliky Ustyug niello is very dark with a clear pattern on a gilded background.

The best work of the Veliky Ustiug masters is profoundly national. It shows clearly the creative style of folk masters. While borrowing themes from books or engravings, they introduced elements of folk art into the treatment of the characters which they depicted.

The finest niello craftsman in Veliky Ustyug was M.Klimshin, who was even invited to Moscow to "raise the level" of niello work there. Another master, A.Moshnin, who made use of engravings and book illustrations, was also well known. He was the first to produce niello views of Veliky Ustyug. The snuffbox in the shape of a book was made by him. On the top is a man sitting in front of an open book, on the bottom an everyday scene of two men in European clothes inviting a peasant in Russian dress to take a pinch of snuff.

At the end of the 18th century the silversmiths in the Veliky Ustyug area turned to the theme of their native towns and plans of them. Note the snuffbox by I.Zhilin with a plan of St Petersburg and the statue of Peter the Great. Zhilin was the founder of a whole dynasty of talented Russian silversmiths. The work of several generations of this family is known.

Eighteenth-century niello work from Veliky Ustyug is characterised by a variety of form in the articles and the refinement of the fine niello engraving. The masters used a number of new technical devices, such as a lowered and flatly chased background to which carved or chased gold and silver details were added. All this makes 18th-century Veliky Ustyug niello work stand out not only in Russia, but also in Europe as a whole.

73

74

☐ **73. Snuffbox.** *Russia, Veliky Ustyug, 18th century. Master: A.Moshnin. Silver; carving, niello. Height 2.4, length 9, width 5.4*

☐ **74. Snuffbox.** *Russia, Veliky Ustiug, 1796. Master: I.Zhilin. Silver; carving, niello, chasing, gilding. Height 2.1, diameter 8.8*

□ **75. Tray.**
*Russia, Veliky Ustyug, 18th ce
tury. Copper;
enamel. Length
14, width 13*

The flowering of jewellery-making in Veliky Ustyug came in the second half of the 18th century, when the town replaced Solvychegodsk as the leading trading, industrial and cultural centre in the Russian North. From the 1760s the unusual technique of coloured and white enamel on a copper base with silver and gold applique work became widespread.

In 1761 Afanasy and Stepan Popov opened a factory which existed until 1776. The factory specialised in niello work, but also produced objects decorated mainly with white or blue enamel with a stamped silver ornament. The articles from this factory — small caskets, perfume bottles and snuffboxes — were usually adorned with niello representations of gallant scenes, pastoral idylls, knights jousting and landscapes with people.

The factory specialised in niello, but also produced articles covered mainly

☐ 76. *Tea service of D.I.Chicherin, Governor of Tobolsk. Russia, Tobolsk, 1774–1775. Silver, wood; carving, chasing, niello, casting, flat chasing, gilding. Height of kettle 30.5, height of coffee-pot 18, height of beaker 10.8*

76

th white or blue enamel and a silver mped ornament.

e decree on the opening of the fac-ry read in part as follows: "Following e request of Afanasy and Stepan pov, merchants of the town of Veliky tyug, it is hereby ordered that ... the d Popovs shall be permitted to set up iligree factory in their houses in the wn and produce ... various curious jects ... made of filigree on copper th applied silver and gold grasses ... th the highest mastery."

e art of niello spread from Tobolsk other Siberian towns. We know of ello-decorated articles made in msk and Yakutsk which are similar those of Tobolsk.

e work of the Veliky Ustyug artists d a great influence on the artistic ntres of Northern Russia, such as logda, Vyatka and Archangelsk. The of niello was carried into the towns Siberia. The availability of orna-

mental materials promoted the development of arts and crafts in Siberia. Here you could buy gold from Bukhara and China and precious stones.

The 1770s saw the flowering of niello work in the Siberian town of Tobolsk, a short-lived but vivid phenomenon. For the most part the Tobolsk craftsmen repeated the subjects of the Veliky Ustyug masters in their work: hunting scenes, local landscapes, town plans, maps, etc. A fine example of this is the tea service which belonged to the governor of Siberia, D.I.Chicherin. The sugar bowl, milk jug, candlesticks and tongs bear the governor's initials and coat-of-arms and the figures of ladies and gentlemen in 18th-century costume.

In the 19th century the production of niello articles in Veliky Ustyug and Tobolsk gradually declined, unable to compete with the large manufactories in Moscow and St Petersburg.

Showcase 18	GOLD AND SILVERWARE – LAST QUARTER OF 18TH TO FIRST THIRD OF 19TH CENTURY

The rococo style did not predominate for long in Russia. By the 1770s whimsical rocaille and sumptuous asymmetrical ornament were being replaced by the flower garlands, laurel and oak branches, symmetrical patterns executed in casting and low-relief chasing characteristic of classicism. This artistic trend arose on the basis of a reworking of the forms of ancient classical art, interest in which had been aroused by the excavations at Heraculaneum (1719) and Pompei (1748). Showcase 18 contains two silver dishes executed by A.Ratkov in 1787. Stylistically they come between rococo and classicism. The smooth even surface of the base, the band of small pearling and the double row of stylised leaves suggest that the master was familiar with the new fashion. However, the sumptuous pattern of bunches of fruit and flowers along the broad edge shows that he had not abandoned rococo completely. Our museum possesses twenty of the thirty-eight surviving works by this fine Moscow goldsmith.

In the 1790s bright, colourful enamel was replaced by two-coloured enamel in two cold shades (known as grisaille). A.Ratkov's chalices and two Gospel covers are adorned with pale blue enamel. Precious stones, such as brilliants, aquamarines and amethysts, were selected to match the cold tones of the enamel.

The gold cup of the chalice made by the Moscow master C.Müller in 1789 is covered with intricate filigree fastened by small diamonds; larger diamonds frame the two medallions of greyish-blue enamel. The chalice is decorated with almost two hundred brilliants of the "first water".

A fine specimen of strict classicism is the oval gold platter by François Séguin (1788) which Empress Catherine the Great presented to Prince Grigory Potemkin for the capture of Ochakov. Round the rim of the plate is an inscription which reads: "To the Commander of the Yekaterinoslav land and sea forces and builder of warships." In the centre is an applied laurel wreath. By combining matt and polished gold the craftsman skilfully brought out the texture and natural beauty of the metal.

It was on this platter that Catherine presented Prince Potemkin with a dia-

77

□ **77. Gospel.** *Moscow, 1806. Master: A.Ratkov. Silver, diamonds; gilding, chasing, enamel. Height 53, width 36*

78

□ **78. Chalice.**
*Moscow, 1789.
Master: C.Müller.
Gold, brilliants;
casting, chasing,
enamel, filigree.
Height 29.5,
diameter of cup
15.4*
□ **79. Dish.**
*Moscow, 1787.
Master A.Ratkov.
Silver; chasing.
Length 71.3,
width 61*

79

80

mond-studded sword. His heirs later made a gift of the platter to the Assumption Cathedral of the Moscow Kremlin.

In this case you can see one of the first Russian samovars made by the Petersburg masters H.Unger and H.Eckert in 1801. Its form reminds one of an ancient Greek amphora. The smooth polished surface is decorated with gold beads of pearling. Next to it are two children's tea services made by the Petersburg master J.Blom, presents from Catherine the Great to her grandsons. The apparent simplicity of the objects executed in classical style in no way affected their material value. The gold Gospel cover by the Petersburg master H.Unger (1794) is embellished with diamonds, aquamarines, amethysts

82

□ **82. Samovar.**
St Petersburg,
1801. Masters:
H.Unger,
H.Eckert. Silver;
chasing, casting,
gilding. Height 50
□ **83. Platter.** St
Petersburg, 1788.
Master: F.Séguin.
Gold; chasing,
casting, carving.
Length 88, width
37.5. Gift from
Empress Cather-
ine the Great to
Prince
G.Potemkin

30. Tea service. St Petersburg, 1784. Master:
Jom. Silver; chasing, casting, carving, gilding.
meter of tray 30
31. Chalice. Moscow, 1797. Master: S.Kuzov.
er, gems; chasing, casting, enamel. Height 33

83

☐ **84. Snuffbox.** St Petersburg, 18th century. Master: G.Ador. Gold, gems; enamel. Portrait of Empress Catherine the Great by K.Geyer. Heigh 1.9, diameter 8

84

and light sapphires, 3,417 precious stones in all.

Snuffboxes of various types became fashionable about this time. Jewellers often decorated them with enamel miniatures. A fine specimen of Russian classicism is the gold snuffbox by a first-class master of that day, the Petersburg jeweller G.Ador, who worked at the court of Catherine the Great from 1762 to 1784 and the Danish artist K.Geyer, who painted the miniature of Catherine.

☐ **85. Gospel.**
*Print – Moscow,
1698; cover St
Petersburg, 1794.
Master: H.Unger.
Silver, gold,
gems, wood,
fabric; casting,
carving, enamel,
gilding. Height
53, width 38.5*
☐ **86. Snuff-
box.** *St Peters-
burg, early 19th
century. Master:
O.Keibel. Gold,
silver, gems;
chasing, carving,
enamel. Length
9.5, width 2.9*

85

86

Showcase 19	**GOLD AND SILVERWARE – LAST QUARTER OF 18TH TO FIRST THIRD OF 19TH CENTURY**

At the end of the century artistic casting of gold, silver and platinum became widespread. The stands of many goblets, vases and candlesticks were cast in the shape of angels or female figures dressed in Greek robes with soft free folds. Thus, the cup of the silver chalice made by the Moscow master S.Kuzov in 1797 is supported by three cast female figures, the stand of the gold cup made by the Moscow master J.Kragge in 1809 is shaped like a female figure and the two small silver candlesticks take the form of a weeping youth and maid in Russian national costume.

The Patriotic War of 1812 was, of course, reflected in applied art. Such untraditional subjects for Russian decorative art as cannons, shells, spears, banners and cannon-balls, infantry- and cavalrymen and eagles on military trophies appeared on objects.

In the 1820s and 1830s many views of Moscow and St Petersburg appeared on silverware and continued to be depicted up to the end of the 19th century, which testifies to people's interest in everything connected with the idea of their homeland and native town.

In this case you can see a platter made by a Moscow master in 1814, which was presented to a hero of the war of 1812 who fought in the Battle of Borodino, the ataman of the Don Cossack host and famous general of the Russian army, Count M.I.Platov, from the Cossack village of Mikhailovskaya. In the middle is Count Platov's monogram and under it his coat-of-arms and the decorations which he was awarded. On either side are banners, cannons and shot. On the left of the chased monogram is a cap with a diamond pen, which Count Platov received for his services in the Patriotic War of 1812. Along the rim of the platter are chased laurel branches. There is a niello presentational inscription on smooth bands of silver around the broad edge. Several platters of this kind were made and presented to Count Platov at different times. One of them is in the collection of the State Historical Museum in Kiev. It was presented to Count Platov in 1816 by the Society of Novocherkassk Traders.

In memory of the great Russian poet the museum has the two wedding crowns which are said to have been worn by Alexander Pushkin and Natalia Goncharova in 1831. They are made of gilded silver and decorated with balls of blue enamel.

88

☐ **87. Dish.** *Moscow, 1814. Master: A.Grigoriev. Silver; casting, chasing, niello, gilding. Diameter 47. Belonged to Count M.Platov*
☐ **88. Goblet.** *Moscow, 1809. Master: J.P.Kragge. Gold; casting, chasing, carving. Height 57, diameter 42*
☐ **89. Wedding crowns.** *Russia, 1800s. Silver; gilding, enamel, glass. Height 24.4 and 25, diameter 20.3 and 19.3*

Showcase 20

PANAGIAS –
18TH TO 19TH CENTURIES

The pectoral insignia of the higher clergy, panagias, form a collection of their own. A panagia is a small icon which was worn on a chain over clothing. Panagias have been known since ancient times. In the 15th and 16th centuries they consisted of two halves hinged together. On the inside they had Our Lady of the Sign and the Trinity, and on the outside the Crucifixion or the Ascension. Panagias of this kind were called "travelling" panagias.

At the end of the 16th century a new type of very grand panagia appeared in the form of a small icon richly decorated with enamel, pearls and precious stones.

In the 18th century panagias assumed the nature of secular ornaments. The most important things about them now

90

☐ **90. Panagia with chain.** *Russia, 1787–1792. Gold, silver, brilliants, pearls; chasing, carving, enamel, gilding. Height 14.8, width 6.8*
☐ **91–92. Panagia with chain (front and reverse).** *Russia, mid-18th century. Gold, silver, brilliants, rubies; casting, enamel, gilding. Height 22.0, width 13.5*

□ **93. *Clock egg.*** *St Petersburg, House of Fabergé, 1899. Master: M.I.Perkhin. Gold, platinum, silver, diamonds, chalcedon; enamel on guilloche, casting, chasing, engraving, carving. Height with base 27, base 9.6×6.4*

93

826, which had distinguished itself he battle of Navarino under the mmand of Captain M.I.Lazarev , for the first time in the history of Russian fleet, been awarded the St orge ensign. The dark green helio-e is decorated with diamond-stud-gold scrolls.

ther equally fascinating article by Perkhin which you can see here is egg-shaped clock made in 1899 and arkable for its elegance and tech-al perfection. The small diamond d does not move, only the white enamel of the dial actually revolves. These intricate "constructions" were beautifully executed and their forms very elegant.

The Fabergé firm was famous for its enamels with their translucent colours and interesting technique. Its crafts-men were skilled at creating a play of colour (by applying five or six layers and fusing each one in turn). They used up to five hundred shades in their enamels. In 1916 in reply to a request from Carl Fabergé's son Alexander to teach him about enamelling, France's

☐ **94. Heliotrope egg with model of the "In Memory of the Azov" cruiser.** *St Petersburg, House of Fabergé, 1891. Master: M.Perkhin. Gold, platinum, silver, gems; casting, engraving, carving. Height 9.3, length of model 7.0*

94

finest enameller Gouyon exclaimed: "You must be mad! We in Paris are quite incapable of making what you fashion so easily in St Petersburg."

At the beginning of the 20th century M.Perkhin produced a gold model of the first train to run along the Trans-Siberian Railway. The carriages are made of gold and each bear an inscription: "Smoking compartment", "Ladies only", "Gentlemen only", "Mail-car" and "Church-car". The engine is made of platinum with a miniature mechanism inside which sets the train in motion. The engine has a ruby light and the carriages have pieces of rock crystal for windows.

The train fits into a large silver egg supported by three gryphons. The egg is engraved with a map of the Trans-Si-

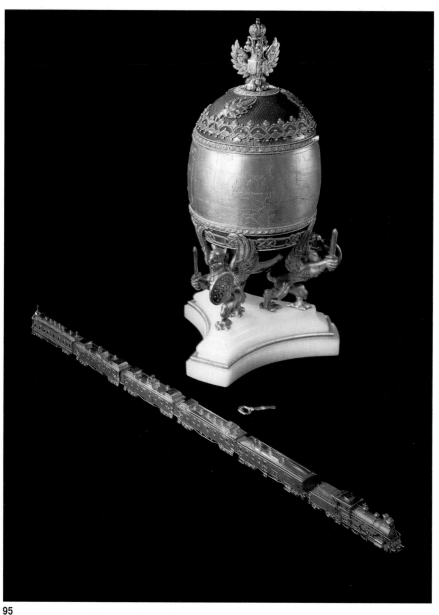

95

☐ **95. *Egg with model of Trans-Siberian Express.***
St Petersburg, House of Fabergé, 1900. Master:
M.Perkhin. Gold, platinum, coloured gold, onyx, crys-
tal; casting, enamel, engraving, filigree, guilloche.
Height 26, length of train 39.8

□ **96. Clover egg.** St Petersburg, House of Fabergé, 1902. Master: M.Perkhin. Gold, platinum, diamonds, rubies; enamel, filigree, chasing. Height with stand 9.8

□ **97–98. Moscow Kremlin egg.** St Petersburg, House of Fabergé, 1904. Master: M.Perkhin. Gold, silver, onyx; casting, enamel, carving. Height with stand 36.1, base 18.5×18.5

96

berian Railway and the year when the already completed part of it was opened – 1900. The upper and lower sections of the egg are covered with green enamel. The egg was exhibited at the World Fair in Paris (1900).

The case contains a small collection of figures carved from crystal, cornelian, onyx, topaz, agate and chrysoprase. Note the crystal vase with a pansy in it. The vase was cut from a single piece of pure, transparent rock crystal, so skilfully turned that the vase seems to have water in it. The flower is made of gold and the leaves and petals are covered with enamel. It was items such as this that made the Fabergé firm so famous.

In the middle of the case you can see a stylised model of the Moscow Kremlin

98

□ **99.** *Fish figurine.* St Petersburg, House of Fabergé, late 19th – early 20th century. Cornelian; carving. 3.5×12.5

100

101

made of coloured gold and silver by the firm's masters in 1904. It is a music box. In the centre is the dome of the Assumption Cathedral. If you look through one of the windows in the church you will see the iconostasis and icons of the Assumption Cathedral. **M**.Perkhin's apprentice and assistant Henrik Wigström made a gold model of the royal yacht "The Standard" which belonged to the tsar's family. The yacht fits into a crystal egg supported by dolphins made of lapis lazuli. **A**fter M.Perkhin's death in 1903, the firm's head jeweller was Henrik Wigström, who in 1913 created an Easter egg commemorating the tercentenary of the Romanov dynasty. **T**he egg is decorated with eighteen miniature portraits of representatives

□ **100. Egg with portraits of Nicholas II's children** *(and model of Alexandrovsky palace inside). St Petersburg, 1908. Master: H.Wigström. Gold, silver, brilliants, rubies, jade; enamel, casting, chasing. Height 11, height of model 3.0, length of model 6.5*

□ **101. Egg with model of "Standard" yacht.** *St Petersburg, House of Fabergé, 1909. Master:*

H.Wigström. Gold, lapis lazuli, silver, brilliants, pearls, rock crystal; enamel, chasing, engraving. Height with stand 15.3, length of model 7.5, height of model 2.0

□ **102. Egg with model of Alexander III monument.** *St Petersburg, House of Fabergé, 1910. Gold, platinum, diamonds; casting, chasing. Height with stand 15.5, base 11.5×11.5*

103

of the reigning dynasty framed with small diamonds.

The egg is on a stand made up of three heraldic eagles fixed to a miniature copy of the state shield made of purpurine. Inside is a revolving steel globe, on which there are two gold appliqué representations of the northern hemisphere showing the territory of Russia, one within the borders of 1613 in coloured gold and the other within the borders of 1913.

The Fabergé firm's last piece of work (1916) is the egg made of steel by H.Wigström whith a base in the form of four shells.

The ability to achieve perfection of artistic form and not only in the quality of the precious materials used is typical of the work by the Fabergé craftsmen.

104

□ **103. Egg with miniature on easel.** *St Petersburg, 1916. Master: H.Wigström. Miniature on ivory V.Zuyev. Gold, steel, jade, ivory; enamel, casting, chasing, water colour. Height with stand 16.7, height of easel 6.5, miniature 5×5.5*

□ **104. Romanov Tercentenary egg.** *St Petersburg, House of Fabergé, 1913. Master: H.Wigström. Miniaturist: V.Zuyev. Gold, brilliants, purpurine; casting, chasing, enamel, painting on ivory. Height 19*

105

106

☐ **105. Dandelion.** *St Petersburg, House of Faberge, late 19th – early 20th century. Gold, diamonds, rock crystal, jade; carving. Height 21.5*
☐ **106. Pansies.** *St Petersburg, House of Faberge, 1904. Master: H.Wigström. Gold, diamonds rock crystal, ivory; casting carving, chasing, enamel, water colour. Height 15.5*

7

□ **107. Clock.** *Russia, late 19th – early 20th century. Master: M.Perkhin. Gold; casting, chasing, enamel, guilloche. Height 12.3, width 11.5*

position as "purveyors to the Court"
ve an austere elite quality to the
m's articles which formed the taste
applied art not only of the crafts-
en, but of the people who commis-
ned these articles as well.

Showcase 21

GOLD AND SILVERWARE – MID-19TH TO EARLY 20TH CENTURIES

As already mentioned, in the second half of the 19th century some large jewellery-making associations were set up in Moscow and St Petersburg which made use of new methods of working precious metals. The owners of these associations employed the top specialists in their workshops, inviting leading artists and historians of art to work for them. In Moscow the firms of Sazikov, Ovchinnikov, Khlebnikov and Semyonov had a high reputation and in St Petersburg – Morozov, Grachev and Fabergé.

This case contains articles made by jewellery firms and factories from the 1830s to the beginning of the twentieth century.

After classicism in art a search began in the 1830s for a new style. Gold and silverware in Russia developed along

108

the lines of mechanically mixing the compositional and decorative elements of all the preceding periods. This resulted in "neo-Gothic", the "second rococo" and "neo-classicism".

The group of objects on the lefthand side of the case are in the "second rococo" style: coffee pots, teapots, sugar basins, milk jugs and sauce-boats decorated with chased scrolls, shells, and applied details.

The passion for naturalist foliate forms can be seen in the sauce-boat shaped like a pumpkin on a leaf and made at the factory of Ivan Gubkin.

In the 19th century in Russia there was a resurgence of interest in mediaeval Russian forms and motifs. The massive silver tankard with twenty-four inset coins and medals is executed in the

109

110

□ **108. Sauce-boat.** *Moscow, I.Gubkin factory, 1894. Silver; gilding, chasing, carving, casting. Height 12.2, length 21.5, width 15.5*
□ **109. Biscuit dish.** *St Petersburg, P.Sazikov firm, 1885. Silver; gilding, chasing, carving, casting. Height 18, length 32.5, width 31*
□ **110. Tankard.** *St Petersburg, 1882. Master: F.E.Henrichsen. Silver; gilding, chasing, carving, casting. Height 47, diameter 19.5*

111

□ **111. "War ior on Guard" sculptural group.** St Peter burg, P.Saziko firm, 1852. Silv casting, chasir carving. Heighi 53, length 58, width 54

Russian tradition. The tankard is engraved with a decree issued by Tsar Alexis in 1661 and the words: "Drink to the bottom in honour of the Tsar". It was made by the Petersburg master F.E.Henrichsen in 1882 for Prince L.A.Lvov.

The large sculptural group of the "Warrior on Guard" on display here was produced by the Petersburg branch of the Sazikov firm founded in 1812. The firm was known for its silver sculpture, which was usually made from models by such famous sculptors as I.P.Vitali and P.K.Klodt. Some of the mediaeval Russian motifs adorning this firm's articles were designed by Academician F.G.Solntsev. Note the lifelike treatment of the horse and warrior. The fine qualities of the sculpture are somewhat

☐ **112. *Sweet bowl.*** *Moscow, 1908–1917, I.Khlebnikov firm. Silver; gilding, filigree, enamel. Height 6, width 14*
☐ **113. *Service.*** *Moscow, V.Semyonov factory, 1880s. Silver; gilding, carving, niello. Height 19.5, 13.3, 8.5*

racted from by the massive stand rned with rocaille scrolls, however. s work is typical of Russian applied in the 1830s to 1850s. It is an inter- ng combination of a mediaeval ssian subject motif and typology h elements of rococo ornament. Ovchinnikov firm founded in 1851 known all over Russia for its

enameled articles. In the case you can see decorative cups, saucers, saltcellars and goblets based on the forms of mediaeval tableware. They are decorated with various types of enamel. The "window" or transparent enamel mastered by the firm is interesting. To obtain this they added water to the enamel, filled the gold or silver "windows" on the article and heated it in a stove. The water evaporated and the enamel fused with the metal, acquiring a transparent quality. Window enamel is very attractive, but did not become widespread due to its fragility. The firm revived the technique of making cloisonné enamel, the secret of which had been lost during the Mongol invasion.

The Khlebnikov firm was famous for its niello work. Some of its articles decorated with niello were displayed at the Industrial Arts Exhibition in 1882. The Semyonov firm specialised in niello alone. Its articles competed with those of the Ovchinnikov and Khlebnikov firms and won awards at international and Russian exhibitions.

Recent acquisitions by the Armoury include the silver tea service made by the Semyonov firm on display here. The items are decorated with niellowork representations of the architectural monuments in the Moscow Kremlin. They were probably based on lithographs of historical monuments and views of Moscow published in the 1850s.

114

☐ **114. Bottle server.** Moscow, A.Ivanov factory, 1908–1917. Silver; casting, chasing, carving, gilding. Height 25

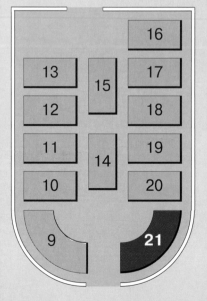

The World Fair of 1889 in Paris showed the features of a new style which became known as "art nouveau". Because of the predominance of flower motifs "art nouveau" in applied art also became known as "floral art".

Flowing plastic figures, smooth curves and patterns of fading irises and watery lines are the hallmark of works created in this style. Examples of it are the glassholders and candlesticks of the Orest Kurlyukov firm and the silver service from the Nemirov-Kolodkin factory.

This large section of Russian decorative and applied art in the Armoury ends with items from Moscow and St Petersburg firms. No other museum in our country has such a rich collection. The craftsmen who created these genuine works of art possessed a brilliant technique, a remarkable feeling for the material and perfect artistic taste.

115

116

□ **115. Service.**
*Moscow,
N.Nemirov-
Kolodkin factory,
1899–1908.
Height of creamer
10, diameter of
saucer 7.5, height
of cup 7.5, height
of sugar bowl
14.5*
□ **116. Punch
bowl.** *Russia, late
19th – early 20th
century. Silver,
crystal; chasing,
carving. Height 46*

HERALDIC TRELLIS

We shall now make our way to the Round Hall. It is separated from the other rooms by a fine openwork iron gate known as the Heraldic Trellis. In the middle is the state emblem of the Russian Empire and around it the emblems of the oldest Russian towns.

Ever since very early times there have been special symbols, insignia, which in the 11th and 12th centuries began to turn into coats-of-arms among European noble families.

These coats-of-arms were composed according to special rules and assigned to states, cities, principalities, families and individuals. A whole special branch of knowledge grew up known as heraldry, which deals with the origin, recognition and composing of coats-of-arms.

In the late 14th and early 15th centuries the figure of a horseman armed with a spear began to appear on the seals of the grand princes of Moscow. It first appeared on the seal of Dmitry Donskoi's son, Vassily (1389–1425), then on the seal of his son Vassily and grandson Ivan III. Thus, the figure on the seals of the Moscow grand princes acquired an hereditary nature and became a coat-of-arms, although officially coats-of-arms did not exist in Russia until the 17th century.

Under Ivan III another emblem appeared on the seals of the grand princes of Moscow, namely, the double-headed eagle. Its appearance on Russian seals was connected with Ivan III's marriage in 1472 to the Byzantine princess Zoya Palaeologina, the niece of the last emperor of Byzantium, Constantine XI Palaeologus.

Considering himself to be the legitimate successor to the Byzantine Imperial house which fell to the Turks in 1453, Ivan III took over the Byzantine state emblem bearing a double-headed eagle, a symbol of the Eastern and Western parts of the Roman Empire which in the first few centuries A.D. was regarded as united. This unity found expression in the emblem – the eagle has a single body and two heads. Thus, the Russian state emblem appeared during the period of the formation of a centralised state and consisted of two main symbols; the horseman slaying a dragon with his spear (from the end of the 14th century) and the double-headed eagle (from the end of the 15th). In the second half of the 17th century these symbols began to be officially regarded as a state emblem.

The horseman and the double-headed eagle on the Russian state emblem underwent certain minor changes be-

tween the 17th to 19th centuries. From the reign of Tsar Alexis the eagle's wings were shown raised upwards and it held a sceptre and orb in its claws. After the institution of the Order of St Andrew the First-Called in 1699 the shield with the horseman on it was always framed by the Order's chain. Following a decree in 1822 the emblems of the realms of Kazan, Astrakhan, Siberia, Poland, the Crimea and the grand duchy of Finland began to appear on the eagle's wings.

In 1856 the emblem was redesigned in accordance with the rules of West-European heraldry (all living figures had to be facing right, i.e., left if you are looking at them, so the horseman began to face left).

The state emblem of the Russian Empire on the gate is surrounded by the coats-of-arms of the oldest Russian cities. The granting of coats-of-arms to cities began in the 1720s in Russia. However, the main cities of mediaeval Russia, such as Moscow, Kiev, Vladimir, Chernigov, Novgorod, Yaroslavl and Smolensk already had their emblems in the 17th century. Emblems from the ancient seals of these cities found their way to the city coats-of-arms. Thus the seal of the Moscow princes bore a horseman slaying a dragon with his spear, which later became the city's coat-of-arms.

The designing of new coats-of-arms was the task of the Heraldic Office set up by Peter the Great. The first Herald Master was Stepan Kolychev. In 1724 Francisco Santi, a Piedmontese nobleman and artist who had studied in Paris, was appointed to assist him. Santi's name is connected with the design of coats-of-arms for nearly all the large Russian towns.

On Catherine the Great's instructions the herald masters A.A.Volkov and M.M.Shcherbatov did a great deal of work to create coats-of-arms for provincial towns.

In order to compose new coats-of-arms detailed information was first gathered about the town's location, trades and other items of interest.

Ever since the time of Kievan Russia our ancestors were constantly having to defend their freedom and independence from attacks by invaders. And this is reflected in individual towns' coats-of-arms.

The old town of Ryazan frequently fought the Mongol-Tartar armies and its coat-of-arms shows a prince standing with his sword drawn. This is probably a symbolical image of the folk hero Yevpaty Kolovrat, who resisted the invading armies fearlessly.

The coat-of-arms of the ancient town of Kolomna also reflects the invasions by the Mongol-Tartar khans. It shows

ite pillar with a crown on the top
reminder of these events.

ne time Smolensk was a border
n of the Russian state and its
nsfolk were constantly concerned
ut its defence, so the town's coat-
rms shows a cannon with a bird of
dise sitting on it.

coat-of-arms of Sergiev Posad
of the famous defence of the
astery-fortress against Polish
ps at the beginning of the 17th
ury. The defenders bravely en-
d the long siege, which explains
the coat-of-arms shows a fortified
with a closed gate, a tower and
pole-axes.

interesting specimen from the time
e Russian opening up of Siberia is
old coat-of-arms of Tobolsk. It
vs a pyramid with banners, drums
halberds. In the 19th century it
redesigned with a Cossack orb and
ld of Yermak between two crossed
ners on a gold background.

coat-of-arms included specific
ures of the geography, economy
life of the particular town.

rly all the coats-of-arms of Siberi-
owns show fur-bearing animals,
ause Siberia was the centre of the
trade in Russia.

example, the coat-of-arms of
tsk has a beaver with a sable its
th.

On the territory of the middle Volga in
the vicinity of Nizhny Novgorod the
cult of the deer has existed since ancient times, and the deer was later included in the city's coat-of-arms.
Two anchors and a sceptre, symbols of
the port and capital, are shown on the
coat-of-arms of St Petersburg.
Saratov province was famous for its
fish, so there are three sterlet on the
town's coat-of-arms.
The coat-of-arms of some towns is
connected with legends about the
town's founding. The Yaroslavl arms,
for example, show a bear with a halberd over its shoulder. Legend has it
that in 1025 Grand Prince Yaroslav,
son of Vladimir, fell behind his retinue
in a dense forest on the right bank of
the Volga, not far from its confluence
with the River Kotorosl. A bear appeared out of a ravine and attacked
him, but the prince killed it with his
halberd. In memory of this event the
prince gave orders for a fortress to be
built on the spot and named Yaroslavl
after him.
Another legend says that on the spot
where Kazan now stands there were
once many dragons, so the city's coat-
of-arms includes a winged dragon.
The coat-of-arms of Tula, famed for
producing Russia's munitions, consists
of three crossed swords and two hammers.

ROOM 4

RUSSIAN ARMS OF THE 12TH TO EARLY 19TH CENTURIES

The collection of ceremonial and hunting firearms and side-arms occupies a considerable place in the museum's collection and is one of the largest in the world. Most of the items are connected with important historical events in the life of the Russian state and belonged to famous military commanders and statesmen, such as Dmitri Pozharsky, Bogdan Khitrovo, Peter the Great and his associates, and also Charles XII, Stephan Bathory and others.

The specifically national features of the Russian armourers' art developed over many centuries. The craftsmen demonstrated great inventiveness in perfecting the fighting qualities of the weapons which were to serve as a reliable defence against foreign invaders.

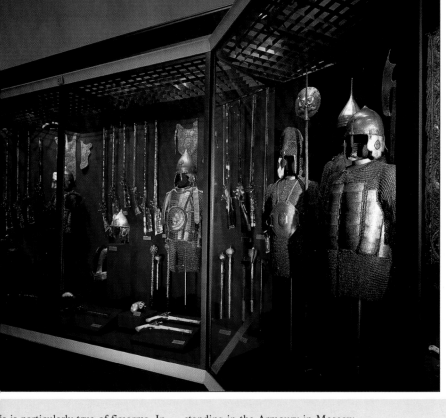

is is particularly true of firearms. In
16th century the Russian forces
sessed some extremely powerful
arms for the day. The English am-
sador Sir Giles Fletcher, who visit-
Russia in 1588, wrote in his book
the Russe Commonwealth" that
other Christian ruler had such re-
ves of military weapons, as could be
n from the large number of cannons

standing in the Armoury in Moscow,
all made of copper and very splendid".
Another European traveller who visited Russia wrote: "..The arsenal is so
big and so richly equipped that it could
arm twenty thousand horsemen..."

Showcases 27, 28

RUSSIAN ARMS OF THE 12TH TO 17TH CENTURIES

The 17th century witnessed the flowering of Russian arms-making. Many fine specimens of weapons have survived which testify to the skill of Moscow craftsmen, who created their own style in firearms. The harquebuses made by them were of complex construction and excelled many produced in the West.

In those days Moscow was the centre of arms-making, with its own specific school. Skilled craftsmen came here from Pskov and Novgorod, the banks of the Dvina and the Volga to learn the armourer's craft.

Russian arms were famed not only for their fighting qualities, however. The weapons and equipment made by such distinguished craftsmen as Nikita Davydov, Ivan Lyamin, Dmitri Konovalov and Grigory Vyatkin are rightly considered to be masterpieces of applied art. In the showcases of this room you will find rare specimens of mediaeval weapons richly decorated with gold, silver and mother-of-pearl. In form, embellishment and artistic and technical execution many of the

117

☐ **117. Helmet.** *Russia, late 12th - early 13th century. Iron, silver; forging, chasing, carving, gilding, silvering. Diameter 19.5.*
Belonged to Prince Yaroslav Vsevolodovich

exhibits in this section of the Armoury are quite unique.

The showcase contains suits of armour, sidearms and firearms used by Russian warriors from the 12th to 17th centuries.

In those days the outcome of a battle could depend in part at least on single combat, so armour, a helmet and a sword were essential to protect the

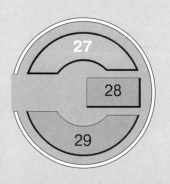

8. Baida-
ussia, late
entury. Iron;
g.
ged to Tsar
Godunov

118

ior. The most widespread type of
nsive armour in Old Russia was
n-mail, a kind of coat made of
l interlaced iron rings.

process of making chain-mail was
emely laborious and sometimes
lved riveting up to twenty thou-
rings. The weight of the coat
d from ten to seventeen kilo-
ns.

The chain-mail which you see in the
lefthand section of the case has an interesting history. It originally belonged
to Prince P.I.Shuisky, Ivan the Terrible's military commander, as can be
seen from the plate on it. In 1564 Shu-
isky was killed at Orsha and the chain-
mail went into the royal treasury. Ivan
the Terrible later presented it to Yermak Timofeyevich, the Cossack leader

who began the conquest of Siberia for Russia. After Yermak's death it was handed over to the Armoury.

Another type of chain-mail is the *baidana*, the rings of which are flat and larger. Chain-mail was sometimes decorated with ornament and inscriptions. The exhibits include a rare specimen of *baidana* chain-mail, which belonged to Tsar Boris Godunov. Each ring is inscribed with the words "God is with us, so none can be against us".

Russian warriors also wore combined armour made of plates and rings, such as the *bakhterets* and *yushman*. Here you can see a *bakhterets* which belonged to Tsar Michael and was made by Konon Mikhailov, a fine Armoury craftsman, in 1620. Russian armour was extremely light, flexible and reliable.

The Armoury possesses a large collection of military helmets. The oldest is the helmet of Prince Yaroslav, father of Alexander Nevsky, the great Russian statesman and military leader who defended north-west Russia against the Swedes and Germans (1240–1242). The helmet was made by skilled Vladimir craftsmen in the 12th century and originally belonged to Prince Mistislav Yurievich. In this helmet Prince Yaroslav fought in the Battle of Lipetsk between the Novgorodians and Suzdalians in 1216 on the bank of the River Koloksha by the town of Yuriev-Polsky. It did not save the prince from being defeated, however. His army was routed and he himself fled from the battle-

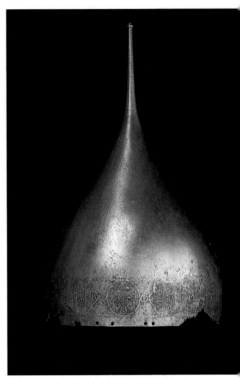

119

☐ **119. Helmet.** *Moscow, 1557. Steel; forging, embossing, chasing. Diameter 18.3. Belonged to Tsarevich Ivan Ivanovich*
☐ **120. Pistols.** *Armoury, first quarter of 17th tury. Master: P.Isayev. Steel, wood, mother-of-pearl; forging, carving, inlay. Length 58*

field, after burying his helmet and armour in the ground. They were found almost six hundred years later, in 1808, by a peasant girl under a hazel tree and taken to St Petersburg. As you can see, the helmet is badly damaged. All that remains are the silver-gilt plates with inscriptions. The armour was buried under the helmet and turned into a heap of rusty rings.

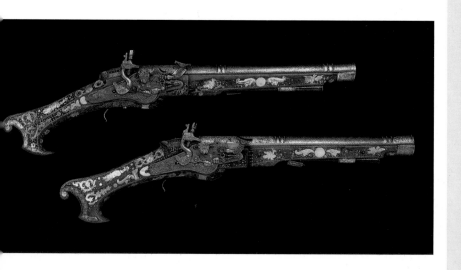

/pical specimen of a Russian hel-
of the 14th to 16th centuries is the
commissioned by Tsar Ivan the
ible for his three-year-old son
ι. It is conical in form with a long
.e. Along the bottom are small
·s for attaching the piece of chain-
ι which protected the neck and
ulders.

main types of sidearms in Old
sia were the boar-spear (a spear
ι a long shaft), the axe, the mace
hort staff or iron rod, with a big,
ılly spherical head), the *shestoper*
ype of mace with six plates or
thers" on the end instead of a
·re, the Russian word *shestoper*
ıns "six feathers"), the *pernat* (a
of *shestoper* with different number
lates), the *berdysh* (a long, broad
with a blade in the form of a half-
on a long shaft), the spear, the
·d and the sabre.

the lefthand side of the case is the
·-spear of Prince Boris Alexan-

drovich of Tver. The tip is made of
damask steel and bound with silver
finely engraved with eight historical
scenes depicting the death of Prince
Michael of Tver on a visit to the Gold-
en Horde.

In the 16th and 17th century the Armoury was the most important of all
the workshops in the Moscow Kremlin. The collection of items made by
the Kremlin armourers in this showcase is not particularly large, but nevertheless testifies to the fine art of
Russian craftsmen.

Here you can see a harquebus made
by Filipp Timofeyevich for the boyar
Bogdan Matveyevich Khitrovo. And
beside it a hunting harquebus made in
1673 by the craftsman Vasily Titov.
Here also are two harquebuses which
belonged to Tsar Peter the Great, one
made in 1688, the other in 1692. By
that time Russian armourers were already making barrels with a series of
spiral grooves as in modern rifles.

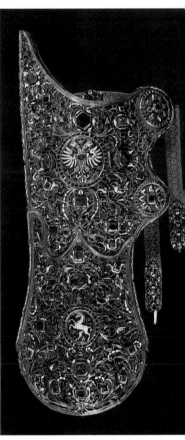

121   122

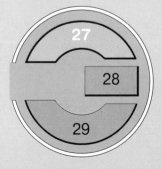

The Armoury possesses about three hundred firearms made by Kremlin masters. In their hands the barrels, locks and butts were transformed into real works of art.

They showed remarkable inventiveness and imagination in the execution of powder canisters, cocking-pieces, flintlocks and springs. In their hands these seemingly prosaic parts of the

□ **121–122.**
Bow case and
quiver. *Armoury,*
1627–1628.
Leather, gold, sil-
ver, gems, fabric;
carving, enamel.
Length of bow
case 78.4, quiver
47.5
□ **123. Helmet.**
Armoury, 1621.
Master:
N.Davydov. Steel,
gold, gems,
pearls; chasing,
carving, emboss-
ing. Diameter 22.
Belonged to Tsar
Michael Romanov

123

-lock took on the forms of fantastic kes, dragons, fish, wild beasts and nsters. The barrels of ceremonial I hunting firearms were decorated h carving, chasing and gilding and butts inlaid with mother-of-pearl, er plating and ivory. nting was a favourite pastime at the al court. The hunts were very sump- us and noisy with lots of people. ishly adorned firearms comple- ited the rich dress of those taking t. An essential item in the equip-

ment was a *saadak*, a special case for a bow and arrows. Here you can see several 17th-century specimens of this kind. Note the splendid case fashioned by Armoury craftsmen for Tsar Michael Romanov in 1628. It is made of gold decorated with enamel and precious stones.

This showcase also contains items by the fine craftsman Nikita Davydov who worked in the Armoury for over fifty years and can rightly be called the father of Russian arms-making. Born in the town of Murom, he learnt his craft from Constantinople armourers and was not only a highly skilled master, but also a talented teacher who trained many gifted armourers.

One of Nikita Davydov's finest items is the ceremonial helmet of Tsar Michael Romanov, which you can see in the centre of the case. It is said to have belonged to Prince Alexander Nevsky. In 1621 Nikita Davydov restored the helmet adding pieces to protect the ears and back of the head. The helmet is made of damask steel with smoothly polished sections. It is oriental in form, yet one can sense the hand of a Russian craftsman. The helmet is decorated with gold ornament in which Russian national patterns are combined with stylised oriental ornament. Nikita Davydov skilfully hammers on the design in continuous gold wire over the roughened surface. This technique is known as *damascening*. The gold ornament is complemented by diamonds, rubies and emeralds mounted in raised settings. In its fine technique of execution, sense of proportion and ornament Nikita Davydov's helmet surpasses the works of famous European and Asian armourers.

Other items by Nikita Davydov exhibited in the case are remarkable for their fine design and careful finish, such as the mirror-armour (defensive armour in which the breastplate and back-plate are made of sheets of steel) and the cuirass.

On the left is a most originally fashioned sabre made by an Armoury craftsman, Ilya Prosvit, in 1618. The damask steel blade is decorated with openwork ornament which not only embellishes it, but also reduces its weight without affecting its durability or fighting qualities.

Note the two rather simple sabres in the case. The notches on the blade bear eloquent testimony to the military prowess of their owners. And these sabres did indeed belong to brave men, namely, Kozma Minin, a townsman of Nizhny Novgorod, and Prince Dmitry Pozharsky who led the Russian people's heroic struggle against the Polish-Swedish intervention at the beginning of the 17th century. (There is a monument to Minin and Pozharsky in Red Square by St Basil's Cathedral). For a long time the sabres were kept in the famous Trinity Monastery of St Sergius. They were handed over to the Armoury in the middle of the 19th century.

Russian warrior in suit of battle armour. 17th century

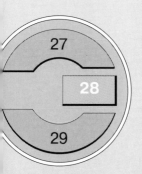

In the 16th and 17th centuries firearms became very widespread in Russia. With their appearance the traditional sidearms lost their military importance and became merely insignia of military authority. In the middle of the room in a showcase of its own (number 28) is a full set of 17th-century armour on a mounted warrior and his horse.

Showcase 29
RUSSIAN ARMS IN THE 18TH AND EARLY 19TH CENTURIES

In the late 17th and early 18th centuries the manufacture of high-quality army and hunting rifles began in Tula, Olonetsk and Sestroretsk. Here you can see an interesting type of hand gun, a mortar that fired small grenades. Here too are some of the rifles used to equip Peter the Great's army. You could say that this showcase is entirely devoted to the age of Peter the Great in Russian history. In the centre you can see a bas-relief of Peter himself by the sculptor Carlo Rastrelli, the father of the famous architect Francesco Bartolommeo Rastrelli. The bas-relief was sculpted in 1741−1743 from tin. If you look carefully at Peter's armour, you can see scenes from the Battle of Poltava on it.

The Northern War for access to the Baltic and independence ended with the brilliant Russian victory at Poltava on 27 June, 1709. This success was the result of the creation of a regular army, well-trained and well-equipped. Here you can see Poltava battle trophies: Swedish drums, kettledrums, signal trumpets, sidearms, firearms and some

personal possessions of Charles XII which he left on the battlefield, including his field Bible and a monogrammed hunting set.

Peter the Great's closest circle included many talented statesmen and military leaders. One of them, Count B.P.Sheremetiev, took part in all the major battles of the Northern War and received the title of field-marshal. The gold keys exhibited in the case were presented to him by the magistrate of Riga following the liberation of the city from Swedish troops in 1710. The keys are most impressive not only in appearance, but also in their weight. Each of them weighs 620 grammes.

In the 18th century Russian sidearms and firearms were manufactured in Tula, St Petersburg and Zlatoust. Here you can see firearms produced by Tula masters.

These skilled armourers passed on their experience from generation to generation. Their fine, almost lapidary work was rated highly by experts. Tula arms are distinguished by beauty of form and refinement of artistic finish. The barrels and butt-stocks are decorated with silvering and gilding, engraving and chasing, inlay and carving.

As a far-sighted politician Peter the Great realised that Russia needed well-organised arms manufacture. On 15 February, 1712 he issued a decree on the building of arms factories in Tula. Two years later, in January 1714, the factories were ready to begin production.

In the lower section you can see a hunting set made by the St Petersburg

124

□ **124. Bas-relief of Peter the Great.** *St Petersburg, 1741–1743. Sculptor C.Rastrelli. Tin: chasing, casting. Diameter 47.5*

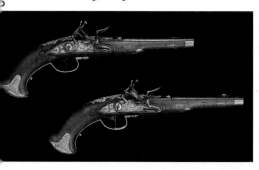

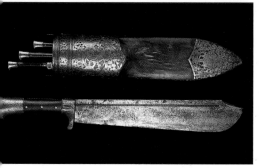

□ **125. Pistols from hunting set.** *St Petersburg, 1770–1780. Master: G.Permyakov. Steel, wood, silver; gilding, engraving, chasing. Length 38.5, calibre 12 mm, length of barrel 23.4*
□ **126. Hunting set with monogram of Charles XII.** *Sweden, late 17th century. Steel, leather; forging, carving. Length of knife 53, length of scabbard 41*

ftsman G.Permyakov at the end of 18th century. Here too are various emonial and officers' swords decoed with silver, gold and precious nes. Swords were sometimes rned with steel "diamonds". The ftsmen polished and faceted small ces of steel until they shone like l diamonds.

ine specimen of the work of the toust armourers at the beginning of 19th century is the sabre fashioned 1829 by the famous craftsman Ivan shuyev, who was nicknamed Ivashko Winged, because he had winged

horses as his hallmark. The blade is burnished and gilded with scenes of the capture of the Varna fortress during the Russo-Turkish war of 1828–1829. On the left is the storming of the fortress and on the right, the entry of Russian troops into the city. The scabbard is decorated with ivory.

Showcase 29
(Continued)

MILITARY ORDERS AND DECORATIONS

The Armoury possesses a collection of Russian military orders and decorations. It is made up of items from the palace property and the chapter of Russian orders. The custom of awarding decorations for military valour existed as far back as the 11th and 12th centuries in Kievan Russia. The recipient was presented with a neck pendant (a decoration in the form of a hoop made of silver, gold, copper or iron). In the 15th and 16th centuries it was customary to decorate all the participants in a military campaign. Other awards in Old Russia included gold and silver vessels and plates, precious furs and rich cloth.

The first order in Russia, that of St Andrew the First-Called, was instituted by Peter the Great in 1698 (see the middle of the case). The order consisted of a star with the motto "For the Faith and Loyalty", a gold chain made up of the state emblems and crosses, and a blue ribbon of watered silk.

The first recipient of the order was Field Marshal Fyodor Golovin. Peter the Great himself was the sixth and received the order in 1703 for capturing two Swedish warships in the mouth of the Neva. The distinguished Russian commanders A.V.Suvorov, P.A.Rumyantsev, M.I.Kutuzov and P.I.Bagration were all decorated with the Order of St Andrew the First-Called.

In 1735 the Order of St Anne with four classes was instituted in Holstein. It was included in the statute of Russian orders in 1797. The order's motto was "To lovers of truth, piety and fidelity". The first class was worn on a broad ribbon over the shoulder, the second on a ribbon round the neck (cf. Chekhov's short story "Anna round the neck"), the third in the buttonhole of a suit, and the fourth on the hilt of a presentational weapon with the inscription "For valour". Only military men were awarded the fourth class. It was the first military officer's decoration.

The highest military award was the Order of St George with four classes, instituted by Catherine the Great in 1769 – a white-enameled gold cross depicting St George and a star with the motto "For service and valour". The first recipient of the first class of this order was Catherine herself. It was a very high award. From the date of its institution up to 1917 the first class was awarded to only twenty-five people, who included Field Marshal P.A.Rumyantsev of the Danube, Prince G.A.Potemkin of the Crimea and the great Russian commanders A.V.Suvorov and M.I.Kutuzov.

In rarity and importance the first class of the Order of St George was higher

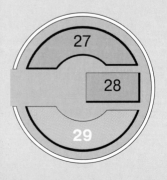

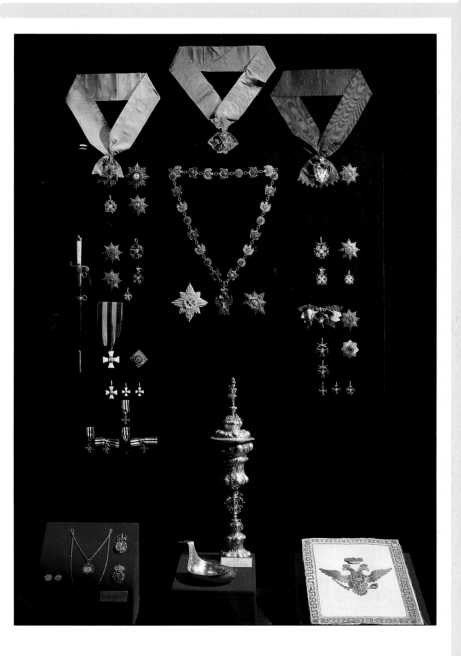

than the state's highest order of St Andrew the First-Called, which was awarded to more than a thousand people.

Next to the Order of St George you can see the St George Cross for soldiers on a striped ribbon. This is not an order, but a decoration. It was instituted in 1807 with one class only, but acquired four classes in 1856. The first and second classes are made of gold, the third and fourth of silver. A soldier awarded this cross was no longer liable to receive corporal punishment. In the First World War officers were awarded the St George Cross for personal valour in battle.

The year 1782 saw the institution of the Order of St Vladimir with four classes – a gold cross with red enamel and a black edge. It was awarded for military and civilian service and for length of service. The order's motto was "Benefit, honour and glory".

There are two Polish orders in the showcase: the White Eagle on a blue ribbon and the Order of St Stanislaw on a red and white ribbon. They were included in the statute in the middle of the 19th century.

Before the revolution orders were awarded only to military, civil and court ranks and the clergy. Peasants and members of the lower middle class were not eligible.

One of the most interesting orders in general is that of St Catherine for women only (not on show in the case)

127

□ **127. Chain and cross of the Order of St Andrew the First-Called.** *Cross. Russia, 1st quarter of 19th century. Gold, enamel; stamping, engraving, guilloche. Hight 12, width 7. Chain. Russia, 1838. Gold; stamping, engraving, enamel.*
Star of the Order of St Andrew the First-Called. *Russia, 2nd half of 18th century. Fabric, pearls, gold thread, paper; embroidery, threading. Diameter 15. Belonged to Empress Catherine the Great*
Star of the Order of St Andrew the First-Called. *Russia, 1st quarter of 19th century. Gold, steel; forging, engraving, enamel. Diameter 12.*

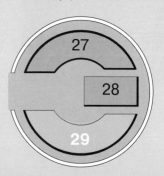

129

hich was instituted by Peter the Great
1714 to commemorate the Prus
ampaign of 1711. The first recipient
the order was the tsar's wife, Cathe-
ne I.

uring the Prus campaign Catherine
d Peter a great service. The Russian
my was encircled by the Turks and
e tsar was in danger of being taken
risoner. Catherine gave the Turkish
ommander-in-chief all her valuables
nd after negotiations Peter's army was
ved. The order's motto is "For love
nd the Fatherland".

ubsequently any lady who received
e order was obliged "...to free one
hristian from barbarous slavery by
uying his freedom with their own
oney". In the 19th century the order
as awarded to court ladies for chari-
ble works.

☐ **128.** *Statute of the Order of St George*
☐ **129.** *Dirk with Cross of Fourth Class of the*
Order of St Anne.
Stars of the order of St Anne.
Crosses of the order of St Anne.
Insignia of the Order of St George. Cross of
First Class. Diameter 6.8, ribbon: width 9, lenth
115
Star. Russia, 1783. Gold; casting, enamel. Diame-
ter 8.1
Belonged to Empress Catherine the Great

ROOM 3   ORIENTAL AND EUROPEAN
CEREMONIAL WEAPONS
OF THE 15TH TO 19TH CENTURIES

Showcases 22, 23, 24   EUROPEAN ARMOUR AND ARMS OF THE 15TH TO 19TH CENTURIES

e Armoury contains specimens of field
d tournament armour, sidearms and
earms made by West European crafts-
en in the 15th to 19th centuries. They
able one to trace to main stages in the
velopment of these types of weapons in
rope over several centuries.

its of armour were usually made to fit
e particular person, the different parts
ing fastened together with straps and
ets. They weighed from 30 to 35 kilo-
ams, so a knight could fight in them
ly on horseback.

e earliest specimen in the Armoury
lection is a 15th-century suit of Ger-
an Gothic armour which is well-pro-
rtioned and beautifully shaped. The
ongated foot-pieces covering the feet
lowed the shape of footwear in that pe-
d. Under the Gothic armour a light
at of chain-mail made of fine inter-
ed rings was worn.

e Maximilian suit of armour dating
ck to the beginning of the 16th century
nteresting. It is named after the Ger-
an Emperor Maximilian (1459–1519)
o is said to have perfected armour: the
ple-like fluting on the plated armour
used enemy swords and spears to
nce off it. The form of the armour
anged in keeping with new fashions in
ess. Rich quilted kaftans influenced the
eastplate and shoulder-piece by making
em curved. The blunt tips of the foot-
ces corresponded to the new fashion
footwear.

the 15th and 16th centuries jousting
mpetitions and tournaments which re-
mbled theatrical performances were
pular in Europe. Tournament armour
s heavier than field armour and, unlike

130

☐ **130. *Gothic suit of armour.*** Western Europe,
late 15th century. Steel; forging, chasing, carving

the latter, adorned with chasing, engraving and gilding. The Armoury has a suit
of 16th-century tournament armour
made in France for a competition on the
ground. The broad plates forming the
skirt did not restrict movement. A tournament was a splendid, striking specta-

cle, but taking part in it was fraught with danger.

The life of a knight who took part in a tournament depended on the stamina and protection of his horse, so the knight would order armour for his horse as well.

The armour made by the famous Nuremberg artistic metalworker Kunz Lochner was very popular in the 15th century. His full suit of ceremonial armour for rider and horse is displayed in a separate showcase. This was a present from King Stephan Bathory of Poland to the Russian Tsar Theodore, son of Ivan the Terrible, in 1584, a fact which is confirmed by the following entry in an archival document: "In the year 1584 on the 22nd of June the ambassador of King Stephan Bathory, Lev Sapiega, made a gift of gilded horse harness and on man".

The armour is adorned with raised medallions of chased mythological figures and what was once gilt ornament.

Apart from the Armoury, Kunz Lochner's work can be found in museums in Stockholm, Dresden, Madrid, Paris and Berlin. It must be said that suits of armour were not used in Russia, but were kept by tsars and boyars as foreign curiosities.

In the showcase you can see some two-handled swords. They are up to one-and-a-half metres long and weigh from 2 to 4 kilograms, so they were held with both hands on a long hilt. The swords with trippled blades possessed great striking

131

☐ **131.** *Maximilian suit of armour.* Germany, early 16th century. Steel; forging, chasing, carving
☐ **132.** *Tournament suit of armour.* France, 16th century. Steel; forging, chasing, carving

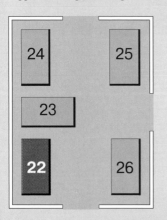

power and were less prone to glance off the surface of armour.

There are several specimens of 15th- to 17th-century firearms on display here. The oldest hand firearm here is a *culevrin* which dates back to the 15th century. The charge was ignited by a long burning fuse like a grass-snake. The gun's name is clearly derived from the French *"couleuvre"*. The simple fuse was replaced by the matchlock, a mechanism for igniting the

133

charge. It existed before the end of the 17th century. At the beginning of the 17th century Dutch muskets equipped with these locks were the main weapons used by the infantry. They weighed from

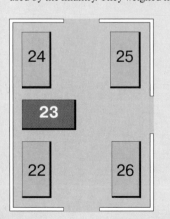

six to eight kilograms, so a stand dug into the ground was placed under the barrel. At the end of the 15th century a new method of igniting the charge appeared, the flint-wheel lock. Its appearance is connected with the name of Leonardo da Vinci, the great artist and scholar of the age of the Renaissance, in whose "Codex Atlanticus" a much improved ignition system, the wheel-lock, was portrayed. The appearance of this new complex construction had important consequences for warfare. Heavy matchlock firearms were used only in the infantry. After the invention of the wheel-lock the cavalry also received firearms. The spring rotated flint wheel was wound up with a key. This was not a good method, because keys are liable to get lost. Nevertheless carbines, pistols and harquebuses appeared with

is kind of lock; thus, short-barrelled
rms of firearms appeared at the begin-
ing of the 16th century.

he pistols (on the left) with a flint-
heel lock made by Nuremberg and
ugsburg masters date back to the end of
ie century.

y the middle of the 16th century, how-
ver, a more reliable way of igniting the
harge had been found, namely, the flint-
harge lock. A spark was produced by the
int striking a piece of steel. The carbine
nd pair of pistols presented to Tsar
fichael Romanov in 1630 by the Dutch
ading agent Carl Demoulin have locks
f this new construction.

rom the second half of the 17th century
o the end of the 18th it was French and
iore specifically Parisian masters who
ood out among the European centres of
rms-making for both technical perfec-
on and artistic mastery.

he Armoury contains works by such
ell-known Parisian masters as Chasteau
id Pirobe. Bertrand Pirobe worked in
ie royal workshop at the Louvre. At the
id of the 18th century presentational
rms were manufactured in the Versailles
orkshops under the supervision of the
insmith Nicolas-Noël Boutet.

1814 the Parisians presented the Rus-
an Field Marshal F.V.Osten-Saken (who
as governor of Paris from 1814 to 1818)
ith a twin-barrelled carbine, a pair of
istols and a sword in a white scabbard

134

☐ 133. *Full suit of ceremonial armour for rider
and horse. Germany, 16th century. Master:
K.Lochner. Steel; forging, chasing, carving*
☐ 134. *Child's suit of armour. Western Europe,
17th century. Steel; forging, chasing, carving*

with a lazurite hilt adorned with a large
diamond. The set was made by
N.N.Boutet at the beginning of the 19th
century. The portrayal of military-heroic
symbols, Greek warriors, gryphons and
eagles was characteristic of the empire
style.

Here too are some hunting rifles and
pocket pistols of the late 18th and early
19th centuries made by English and Bel-
gian masters, who by then held pride of
place in arms making.

Showcase 25

TURKISH ARMS OF THE 16TH AND 17TH CENTURIES

135

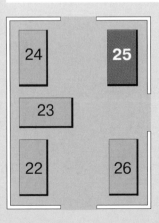

The 16th and 17th centuries saw a strengthening of diplomatic relations and trade between the Russian state and the East and West. Following the etiquette of that time ambassadors and merchants who came to Russia brought rich gifts with them. From oriental countries they usually carried sidearms, jewellery, pedigree racehorses, horse harness, carpets, rich fabrics and spices. Showcases 25 and 26 contain daggers, sabres, shields, bow-and-arrow cases and helmets made in Persia and Turkey in the 16th and 17th centuries. All these

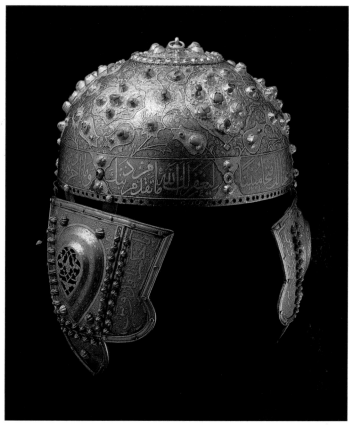

□ **135. Gaunt-
lets.** *Turkey, late
16th – early 17th
century. Steel,
gold, gems, tur-
quoise; chasing,
inlay. Length 39.5*
□ **136. Helmet.**
*Turkey, late 16th –
early 17th century.
Steel, gold,
gems, turquoise;
chasing, inlay,
carving. Diameter
19*

136

•ms have an oriental luxury about
•em. In 1636 merchants from Istam-
•l presented Tsar Alexis with a sabre
•d a bow-and-arrow case. The com-
•nation of emeralds and rubies with
•een enamel is a characteristic feature
' Turkish articles of the period. The
•scription in Arabic on the blade
•ads: "May your time be spent in
•ss." In the middle of the case is a
•uble-headed eagle and a Greek in-
•ription dedicated to Tsar Alexis.
•rkish craftsmen were skilled at inlay-
•g with gold and precious stones such

objects as maces, *shestopers* and *per-
nates* made of rock crystal, jade and
agate.

The helmet and gauntlets of Prince
F.I.Mstislavsky are covered with a
wavy gold ornament of large tulips executed in the damascening technique,
rubies and small bright turquoises.

The reed shields presented by Istambul
merchants to Tsar Alexis are decorated
with jade and silver plates, rubies, turquoise and pearls.

Showcase 26

PERSIAN ARMS OF THE 16TH AND 17TH CENTURIES

□ **137. Shield.** Persia, 16th century. Master: Muhammed Mumin Zernishan. Steel, gold, gems, turquoise, pearls; chasing, carving, inlay, gilding. Diameter 48.8

137

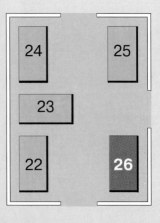

Particularly noteworthy is the 16th-century circular Persian shield which belonged to Prince F.I.Mistislavsky, a military commander under Ivan the Terrible and Boris Godunov. After his death in 1622 the shield was taken into the state treasury. In an Armoury inventory of 1687 it headed the list as an object of exceptional artistic value.

The shield is forged from a single sheet of damask steel and ornamented with pear-like shapes, alternately damascened with gold, and adorned with an elegant pattern of animals and people.

☐ **138. Dagger.**
Blade – Persia, first half of 16th century. Mount – Turkey, 17th century. Gold, jade, gems, steel. Length 20

138

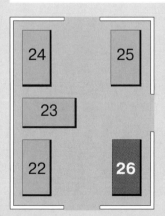

Of special note among the ambassadorial gifts from the shahs of Persia to the Russian tsars in the 17th century is the shield made of rhinoceros skin, decorated with a band of gold and pearls round the edge and a gold medallion with an emerald and rubies in the middle.

Note the small bright dagger. The blade was made by Persian craftsmen in the first half of the 16th century and richly decorated with gold. The mount was the work of Turkish jewellers in the

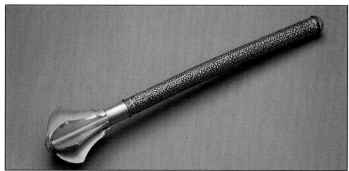

139

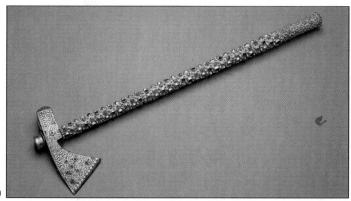

140

□ **139. Pernat.** *Turkey, mid-17th century. Gold; niello, casting, chasing, carving. Length 51.7. Presented to Tsar Alexis by Shah Abbas in 1658*

□ **140. Hatchet.** *Persia, 17th century. Steel, wood, silver, gold, gems, turquoise, pearls; chasing, inlay, flat chasing. Length 66.5*

h century. It is made of jade plates
h rubies and mounted in gold petals
d a fine mesh of intertwining stems.
e *shestoper* with a lacy openwork
idle (far left), a gift from Shah Ab-
. II to Tsar Alexis, is made of pure
d and weighs 1.2 kilograms.
re too you can see a 17th-century
d hatchet and a gold mace from the
rand Regalia" presented to the
ssian Tsar by Shah Suleiman in
)2, which is literally covered with
cious stones.

ROOM 5

WEST EUROPEAN SILVER OF THE 13TH TO 19TH CENTURIES

You are now entering the last room on the first floor of the museum. Here you will find one of the Armoury's largest collections, namely, items made by foreign craftsmen in the 13th to 19th centuries. Most of them came to Russia as ambassadorial gifts. The collection is extremely valuable because it illustrates the national characteristics of the decorative and applied art of many countries and is one of the world's largest collections of West European silver.

At the end of the 15th century, in connection with the formation of the powerful, centralised Russian state, trading and diplomatic relations were set up with the countries of both East and West. And by the end of the 16th century Russia's diplomatic relations with other states had expanded to such an extent that it was found necessary to set up a special Ambassadorial Office, which administered relations with foreign states, sent Russian envoys abroad, organised receptions for envoys in Moscow and supervised matters relating to foreign merchants.

The conclusion of agreements between states, the restoration of lost trading privileges or the announcement of the accession of a new ruler were entrusted to so-called "great" or "grand" embassies. Relations with foreign states were carried on with the help of "light" envoys and messengers. And, of course, once the Ambassadorial Office had been set up and the first diplomats appeared, it became necessary to draw up diplomatic protocol to estab-

lish the procedure for receiving foreign embassies. This protocol remained almost unchanged up to the 18th century.

Great political importance was attached to the meeting and receiving of foreign ambassadors. A special building, the Hall of Facets, was erected in the 15th century for state receptions. Receptions in the Kremlin were extremely sumptuous and attended by many boyars and high officials. The important ceremony of the presentation of credentials was invariably followed by the handing over of gifts by the ambassadors.

According to the etiquette of those days each embassy brought rich gifts. Presents to the tsar from rulers of equal rank were called "loving remembrances", while offerings from the ambassadors themselves were a "petition".

The "grand embassies" brought numerous rich gifts. The success of the negotiations depended to some extent on the value of the gifts presented. In the course of return visits Russian ambassadors in their turn presented foreign rulers with no less sumptuous offerings, sometimes twice as valuable as those received.

This room contains ambassadorial gifts from England, Holland, Denmark, Poland and Sweden.

Showcase 30 — AMBASSADORIAL GIFTS. HOLLAND

□ **141. Pickle dish.** Holland, Amsterdam, first half of 17th century. Silver; chasing, gilding. Height 6.7, diameter 3

141

The ambassadorial gifts from Holland on display here are the work of the finest 17th-century silversmiths from Amsterdam, Utrecht, the Hague and Leyden. They include wall candelabra, jugs, goblets, dishes, plates, candle-trimmers, sugar tongs, etc.

Holland was the first country in Europe to have a bourgeois revolution, which led to the formation of a federative bourgeois republic. This period also witnessed a remarkable flowering of learning and art in Holland. The 17th century was the age of Uriel Acosta, Descartes, Spinoza, Huygens, Hals, Rembrandt and Vermeer, whose work brought immortal fame to this small country.

The applied arts flourished in particular. Articles of silver and ivory and ar-

□ **142. Wall candelabrum.**
Holland, Hague, 1647. Master: H.K.Bregchtel. Silver; chasing, casting, pouncing gilding. Height 91, width 40

142

tic pottery were all part of the life of the rich bourgeoisie. The Dutch craftsmen strove to make their objects not only beautiful, but also of use in everyday life. The items in this show-case are all large and highly decorative they were intended for ambassadori-gifts.

Our museum's collection of Dutch silver consists of one hundred and sixty seven pieces and is made up for the most part of presents from embassies in 1648, 1665 and 1676.
In 1648 a "grand" embassy led by Koenraad Burgh arrived in Moscow. It brought to Russia wine jugs chased

□ **143. Dish.**
*Holland, Amsterdam, 1664. Master: H.T.Huylsen.
Silver; chasing, gilding, pouncing.
Diameter 78*

143

with lobed ornament, wall candelabra and candle-trimmers. The ambassadorial gifts of 1648 also included a silver dish for oysters chased into twenty-four lobes and made by one of Amsterdam's finest silversmiths, Jan Lutma the Elder (c. 1585–1669). Lutma's work is monumental and harmonic. He was the first to use lobed ornament and to make the handle of a vessel in the form of a curved dolphin.

The case contains many wine bowls, vases, goblets and jugs belonging to that "man of distinction" Grigory Dmitrievich Stroganov, as can be seen from the carved inscriptions on them. They were all made by specially commissioned Dutch craftsmen.

As you have probably noticed, many items of 17th-century Dutch silverware

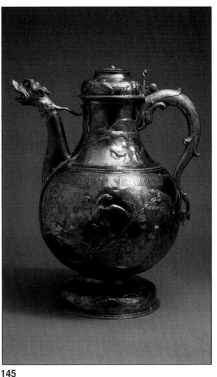

44

□ **144. Winebowl.** *Holland, Amsterdam, 1663.*
Master: R.Pitter. Silver; chasing, casting, engraving,
gilding. Height 25

145

□ **145. Jug.** *Holland, Amsterdam. Master:*
R.Pitter. Silver; chasing, casting, engraving, gilding.
Height 45.5

e decorated with the so-called carti-
ginous ornament which became
idespread in European applied art.
he large silver wall candelabra
rought in 1648 are also adorned with
is type of ornament.
ne gifts brought by the embassy of
565 include a dish by the eminent
utch craftsman Hendrick Tom
uylsen. By the 17th century Holland
as also famed for its flower-growing.
nd alongside the cartilaginous orna-
ent one finds chased stylised tulips
d carnations on many articles, in-
uding this dish. The cultivation of tu-
os brought from Persia began in the

17th century. The bulbs were valued so
highly that they were included in dow-
ries and bequeathed in wills.
Many Dutch merchants traded with
Russia for decades and knew our country well. Some of them even performed
the functions of authorised envoys.
Thus, in 1676 a "large" embassy came
to Russia led by Koenraad van Klenk,
whose family had traded in Russia for
many years. The embassy brought rich
presents with it, including large dishes
with the Russian coat-of-arms on the
bottom and many drinking vessels:
beakers and wine goblets – these were
made and purchased by the dozen.

Showcase 31

AMBASSADORIAL GIFTS. ENGLAND

Among the numerous gifts displayed in this room, the collection of English silver of the 16th and 17th centuries holds pride of place. Such items are not to be found even in England itself, as they were melted down to make coins during the Civil War of 1642–1648. The Armoury possesses about one hundred and thirty articles made by English silversmiths in the 16th and 17th centuries. Most of them were brought to Russia by diplomats, but some were purchased from merchants. Permanent trading and diplomatic relations between Russia and England were set up in 1553. The initiative came from England, which was seeking new markets for its wares. In an attempt to find a northern sea route to India and China, three English merchant vessels sailed round the north of Europe, but the voyage ended tragically when two of them were shipwrecked. The third, under the command of Richard Chancellor, managed with great difficulty to reach the mouth of the Northern Dvina and anchored not far from the place where the city of Archangel was later founded. The arrival of foreign ships on Russian soil was an event of great importance at that time. The leader of the expedition, Richard Chancellor, was received in Moscow by Tsar Ivan the Terrible himself. The Englishman's courage was appreciated by the Russian monarch, and English merchants received the right to trade freely in Russia. This marked the beginning of permanent trading and diplomatic relations between England and Russia. The showcase contains English goblets, wine vessels, jugs, winebowls and plates. The items are characterised by

□ 146. *Pickle bowl.* England, London, 1557–1558. Silver; chasing, casting, engraving, gilding. Height 15.7

146

their gentle lines, clear and precise ornament (a preponderance of low-relief chasing with realistic animals, fish and flowers) and high technical perfection. The earliest exhibit in our collection is a small pickle bowl (mid-16th century), a low vessel of silver-gilt, like a small vase with a shallow, circular bowl. Such bowls were used for serving all sorts of pickled delicacies and sweetmeats, such as candied and marinaded fruit, sweets, nuts and berries. The bowl was presented to Ivan the Terrible by Anthony Jenkinson, one of the first English ambassadors to Moscow.

In the 15th and 16th centuries salt was very expensive in England. The position of the saltcellar on the table determined who sat where. The host and his

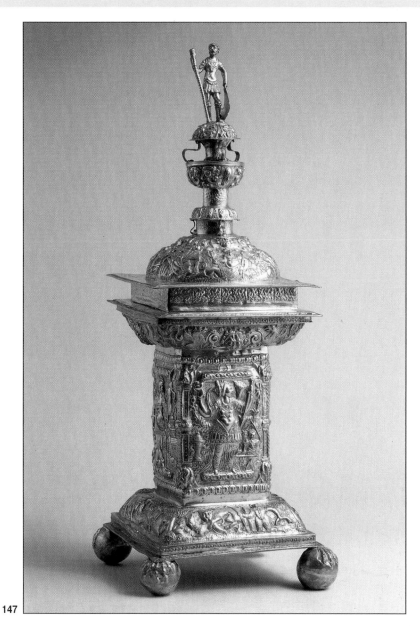

147

☐ **147. Salt cellar.** *England, London, 1594–1595. Silver; gilding, chasing, engraving, casting. Height 40.2*

most honoured guests sat further up the table from it, and the less honoured further down.

The two salt cellars in the middle of the case have an interesting shape. They are far bigger and more decorative than the simple salt cellars of today. These two have a high cylindrical or square body with lids topped by a human figure or pointed turret, a typical English ornament found not only in applied art, but also in the sculptural details of palaces and cathedrals.

On the top shelf of the showcase are two huge ounces, or wine jugs, of chased silver. These masterpieces are the pride of the collection, and there is nothing to match them in any other museum in the world. The ounces were brought to Moscow in 1629 by trading agent Fabian Ulyanov. In fact he received considerable recompense for the ounces: 1,000 roubles and some sable furs.

The Armoury collection contains thirty-two goblets made by English silversmiths. In number and variety of form this collection is also considered the finest in the world. Here you can see

148

spherical goblets decorated with diamond facets, pumpkin-shaped goblets topped with turrets or obelisks, and others.

The collection of pitchers, which were used for washing hands with rose-water after meals, is worthy of note. They

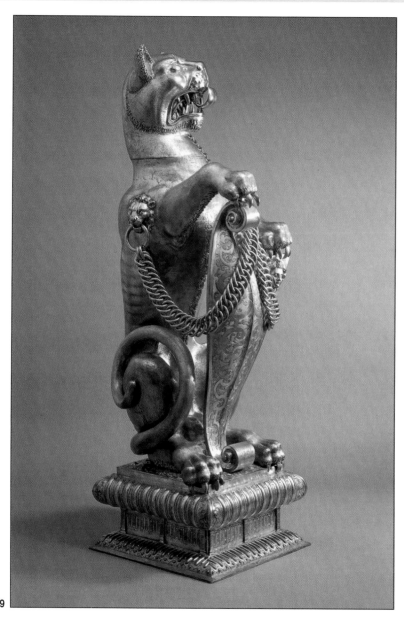

149

☐ **148. Salt cellar.** *England, London, 1611–1612. Master: R.Brook. Silver; chasing, casting, gilding. Height 40*   ☐ **149. Ounce.** *England, London, 1600–1601. Silver; casting, gilding. Height 98*

150

151

were brought to the table with special tubs. In the centre of the showcase are four large egg-shaped pitchers which date back to the beginning of the 17th century. The spouts are in the shape of a dragon with widespread wings and the handles in the form of a coiled snake. There is nothing like them in any other museum. The collection of wine flasks is also unique. Their shape came from the flasks which pilgrims used to carry during the crusades.

In the middle of the 17th century the exchange of embassies between Russia and England was interrupted due to the Civil War. The Assembly of the Land (a congress of representatives of the boyars, the service gentry, the clergy and the rich merchants in Russia during the 16th and 17th centuries) re-

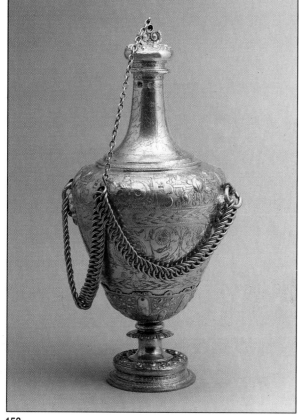

☐ **150. Jug.**
*England, London,
1614–1615. Sil-
ver; casting,
chasing, gilding.
Height 67*
☐ **151. Jug.**
*England, London,
1604–1605.
Silver; chasing,
casting, engrav-
ing. Height 64*
☐ **152. Flask.**
*England, London,
1580–1581. Sil-
ver; chasing,
casting, engrav-
ing, gilding.
Height 44*

152

ved to expel all English merchants
n Russia because they had "put
ir sovereign King Charles to
th".

er the accession of Charles II to the
glish throne a "large" embassy un-
Sir Charles Howard, Earl of Car-
e, accompanied by a suite of a hun-
d people, came to Russia. The em-
sy brought the Russian tsar rich
s, which included silver candle-
ks, goblets and plates. Most of
m can be seen on display here. The
erware brought by Carlisle was
de in 1663 in London. Unlike the

earlier articles by English silversmiths,
these are decorated with bold relief
chasing.

Showcase 32 — AMBASSADORIAL GIFTS. POLAND

☐ **153. Dish.**
*Poland, Gdansk,
mid-17th century.
Silver; chasing,
gilding. Length
128*

153

This showcase contains ambassadorial gifts from Poland, including silverware made by Polish and German craftsmen. Russia's relations with Poland varied. One of the main problems which Russia faced at the beginning of the 17th century was that of regaining the old Russian lands and reuniting the Ukrainian and Byelorussian territory which was ruled by the Rzecz Pospolita (the name of the Polish state in the 16th and 17th centuries when it was united with the Grand Duchy of Lithuania).

In January 1654 at the Pereyaslavskaya Rada the Ukrainian people supported reunion with Russia. In the same year the Russian army liberated Smolensk, Gomel, Mogilev and Vitebsk from the Polish magnates and occupied

Byelorussia and Lithuania. Tsar Alexis of Russia assumed the title of Tsar of all Great and Small and White Russia", i.e., ruler of Russia, the Ukraine and Byelorussia.

In the second half of the 17th century, however, relations between Russia and Poland improved mainly as a result of their joint struggle against Turkey. The "permanent peace" concluded in 1686 did much to strengthen Russo-Polish collaboration.

In the course of the 17th century several Polish embassies came to Russia. The one in 1668 (which invited Tsar Alexis or his son Alexis to become king of Poland) brought silverware made by the masters of Gdansk. The gifts included richly decorated silver jugs and an oval bucket chased with convex lobes (which are on display). On the bottom of the bucket is the mythological scene of Perseus freeing Andromeda.

Here too you can see one of the finest pieces of work by the famous Augsburg silversmiths Abraham I Drentwett and Heinrich Mannlich, a silver one-head-ed eagle with outspread wings, holding a sceptre and orb in its claws. The eagle was brought to Russia in 1671 as a present from King John Sobieski to Tsar Alexis. The disc on the eagle's head may have served as a rest for a crown.

154

□ **154. Bagpipe goblet.** *Poland, Fraustadt, 17 century. Silver; chasing, casting, gilding. Height 38.5*

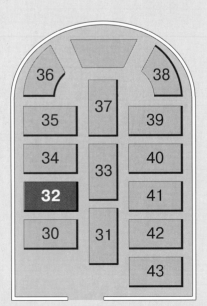

☐ **155.** *Eagle.* *Germany, Augsburg, 17th century.*
Masters: A. Drentwett I and H. Mannlich. Silver;
chasing, casting, gilding. Height 89

Showcase 33

AMBASSADORIAL GIFTS. SWEDEN

One of Russia's closest neighbours in the West was Sweden. In the 17th century the two countries established permanent diplomatic relations. The ambassadorial gifts from Sweden are the most numerous in this collection. There are more than two hundred different plates, wine vessels, wash-jugs, vases and wall ornaments. Silver-making was actually not very developed in Sweden, which explains why most of the items displayed here are the work of 17th-century German craftsmen. **G**erman silverware of this period was famous throughout Europe. Many states bought it to present as ambassadorial gifts. The Swedish court not only purchased works of art in other countries, but also invited foreign masters, artists, architects, sculptors and

156

☐ **156.** *Horn of Plenty goblet.* Germany, Hamburg, 17th century. Master: D. Thor Moye. Silver; chasing, casting, engraving, gilding. Height 67

dsmiths to come and work in Swe-
. .
first Swedish embassy which came
Russia after the Thirty Years War
that of 1647 to congratulate Tsar

Alexis on his accession to the throne.
On behalf of Queen Christina the ambassador Erik Gyllenstjern presented
the tsar with two huge gilded bowls by
Augsburg craftsmen. On one of them is

Biblical scene of the reconciliation
acob and Esau and on the other
capture of Carthage by the Ro-
s. Among the gifts were many
lets, including an original one in

the form of a horn of plenty supported
by a cast figure of the goddess Ceres,
the work of by the Hamburg master
Dietrich Thor Moye (in the middle of
the showcase).

158

159

157

☐ **157. Toilet box.** *Sweden, Stockholm, 17th c*
tury. Silver; gilding, filigree, chasing, casting. He
6.0, diameter 10.4

Russia, which was striving for an out-
let to the Baltic, could not remain in-
different when Sweden occupied
Polish territory in 1654 and took
Lithuania under its protectorate. So
it is not surprising that the embassy of
Gustav Bjelke which arrived at this
time to assure the Russians of Sweden's friendship was unsuccessful, although it presented the tsar with rich
gifts, such as pickle bowls, wash-jugs,
globes and candlesticks in the shape of
female figures (all on display here).
Particularly noteworthy is the table
fountain made by the Hamburg master
Peter Ohr and brought to Russia with
other presents by a Swedish embassy
in 1662 (in the middle of the case at
the top). Water or wine rose under
pressure from the lower section to the

158. *Celes-*
al globe. Ger-
any, Hamburg,
'th century.
aster:
Lambrecht II.
ver; chasing,
sting, engrav-
g, gilding.
ight 64.
ought with gifts
m King Charles
of Sweden in
'55

159. *Beaker.*
veden, Stock-
lm, end of 17th
ntury. Master:
Nutzel. Silver;
asing, casting,
ding. Height 33.
ought with gifts
m King Charles
of Sweden in
199

160. *Wash*
g. Germany,
gsburg, be-
een 1674–
80. Master:
Mannlich.
ight 40.
ought with gifts
m King Charles
of Sweden in
199

160

er one and sprinkled water on
es of fruit from the cluster of silver
s of lightning in Jupiter's hand.
showcase contains a group of arti-
made in Stockholm, namely,
rters for tea and spices, tall smooth
lets, candlesticks and filigree toilet
es. They were brought to Russia in
9 from King Charles XII of Swe-
for Peter the Great.

In spite of the undoubted influence of
German craftsmen, Swedish silverware
has features of its own both in the form
of the articles and in the predominance of certain types of technique,
such as filigree work.

Showcase 34

AMBASSADORIAL GIFTS. DENMARK

161

162

The exhibits in this case are ambassadorial gifts from Denmark, silverware made by German masters in the 17th century.

The growing power of Sweden aroused the concern of its closest neighbour Denmark, whose economic position depended on trade in the Baltic. So the Danish kings did their utmost to ally with the Russian state.

In the 16th and 17th centuries trading and diplomatic representatives from Denmark frequently came to Moscow. Christian IV sought to establish not only official, but also matrimonial ties with the Russian court. In 1602 a "large" embassy arrived in Moscow led by the king's brother John. The embassy had a highly delicate mission, namely, to win the hand of Boris Go-

nov's daughter, Ksenia, for Prince
hn. The prince's sudden illness and
ath put paid to Christian IV's ambi-
us plans.

e Danish monarch showed great
rsistence, however. In 1644 his son
oldemar arrived in Moscow with a
arge" embassy as a suitor for Tsarev-
Irina, the daughter of Tsar Michael
omanov. And again the mission was
successful, this time because the
ince refused to adopt the Russian
thodox faith. Nevertheless the em-
ssy presented the Russian tsar with
merous gifts: ceremonial horse har-
ss, vessels made of mother-of-pearl
d more than two hundred articles
ade of silver. Most of these are dis-
ayed here. They consist mainly of
th-century silverware made by
amburg craftsmen. Here you can see
ckle bowls with a Venus-shaped
m, a goblet in the form of a sliced
elon on a plate of fruit, a deer-
aped pitcher for washing hands and
silver object with small shell-like
ates for sweetmeats, known as a
onfectionery tree".

e Armoury's collection of German
ver consists of about one thousand
ms. German silverware can be found
the museums of Nuremberg, Dres-
n, Vienna, Florence, Paris and St
tersburg, but the Armoury possesses
e of the largest collections of Ger-
an silver from Augsburg, Nuremberg,
amburg, Lübeck, Rostock, Darm-
dt, Passau, Essen, Leipzig and
resden. The development of this art
Germany was promoted by the
despread demand for luxury articles
d the fact that Germany led the
rld in silver mining and processing.
is showcase with ambassadorial gifts
m Denmark contains articles made
masters in various German towns.
te the fumigator executed by Ham-
rg silversmiths in 1600. Aromatic
ots and herbs were placed on red-hot
arcoal, then fragrant oils were

163

□ **161. Melon goblet.** *Germany, Hamburg,
1631–1633. Master: G. Lambrecht II. Silver; chasing, casting, gilding. Height 38*
□ **162. Deer.** *Germany, Hamburg, 1635–1644.
Master: J. Jans. Silver; casting, chasing, gilding.
Height 40*
□ **163. Confectionery tree.** *Germany, Hamburg,
1633–1644. Master: D. Thor Moye. Silver; casting,
chasing, pouncing, gilding. Height 75*

poured on them, which gave off a
pleasant odour under the action of the
high temperature.

Showcase 35   ARTICLES MADE BY NUREMBERG GOLDSMITHS

The main centre of silver-making in Germany until the end of the 17th century was Nuremberg. Already in the 13th century it received the right of an Imperial town and had a well-developed trade and by the end of the 15th century boasted a population of one hundred thousand. The applied arts flourished in the city, particularly jewellery making. The Armoury's collection of Nuremberg silver consists of two hundred and sixty five items and represents the work of a hundred and twenty masters. The Nuremberg goldsmiths made silverware for religious and secular use, but above all they were famed for their goblets.

The collection of goblets by Nuremberg masters on display in the Armoury is extremely varied, covering the peri-

□ **164. Goblet**
*Germany, Nurem-
berg, before
1519. Silver; en-
graving, chasing,
casting, carving,
gilding. Height
35.5, diameter
15.5.
Present from
Boris Godunov to
Patriarch Job in
1589*

164

od from the 15th to 17th centuries. The silversmiths often made their goblets from engravings and drawings by well-known artists, such as Albrecht Dürer, Hans Holbein the Younger and Peter Flötner.

The eminent German artist and engraver Albrecht Dürer received a good training as a young lad from his father, who was a jeweller. His sketches and engravings of goblets and various types of ornament show remarkable precision. Dürer's engravings were known to many silversmiths in Germany. It

□ 165. *Double goblet.* Germany, Nuremberg, 16th century. Silver; chasing, casting, engraving, enamel, painting on glass, gilding. Height 60

□ 166. *Amusement goblet.* Germany, Nuremberg, 1575–1586. Master: J. Heberle. Silver; chasing, casting, engraving. Height 29.3, diameter 9.5

5   166

s thanks to them that goblets ap-
ared in the shape of apples, pears
d pumpkins and the stems of vessels
quired the form of tree trunks en-
ined with vines.

e earliest specimen of the Dürer-
pe of goblet on display is a small sil-
r pear-shaped one presented by the
ssian Tsar Boris Godunov to Patri-
h Job (in the front of the showcase
the end). This goblet was made by
unknown craftsman in the late 15th
early 16th century in the Late
thic style. The surface is chased

with protruberances pointed at the top
and bottom.

The flowering of the applied arts in
Germany was promoted by its proximi-
ty to Italy. German jewellers quickly
adopted the forms of the Italian Renaissance. They too were interested in
the real world and representations of
animals and plants.

A characteristic feature of the new
style was its balanced proportions, horizontal division and clarity of form.
The ornament of this style was incredi-
bly diverse. Craftsmen decorated ob-

jects with masks, vases, torches and "putti", but it was the so-called "Rollwerk" (belted braiding) that predominated.

A splendid example of a Renaissance goblet is the 16th-century double silver goblet on display here, which delights one with its strict proportions and clarity of composition. Each section of the goblet is clearly delineated and adorned with chased mythological scenes. The stem is decorated with an enamelled foliate pattern of birds and the base with medallions on which there are traces of painting under the glass (second shelf from the bottom, on the right).

Double goblets became widespread in the 16th century. At first the upper section was smaller than the lower one and intended for the cup-bearer to taste the wine before serving it at the prince's or tsar's table. Gradually these sections became the same size and acquired a different function. Drinking together from such a goblet during a feast became a token of friendship. Double goblets were also given as wedding

167

□ **167. Eagle.** *Germany, Nuremberg, 1595. Master: C.Jamnitzer. Silver; chasing, casting, gilding. Height 74.5*

presents to symbolise the strength of matrimonial ties.

The articles made by the Jamnitzer family were famous. The head of the family, Wenzel Jamnitzer, was a jeweller, silversmith, engraver and scholar. His art influenced many German masters. Jamnitzer created a goblet in the form of a bluebell which became a kind of test of skill. Any craftsman who was taking the examination for the title of master had to make a bluebell goblet. Only then was his art recognised as worthy of the title.

The Armoury has only one object from the workshop of Wenzel Jamnitzer, a small beaker decorated with a fine ornament of "Rollwerk" (at the end of the showcase on the left).

Wenzel Jamnitzer was also the first to design the main types of Nuremberg goblets with figures of Roman warriors and allegories of the virtues on the lids.

e had many apprentices and follow-
s, whose work is displayed in this
owcase, such as Christoph Ritter I,
ias Lencker, Adam Fischer and Hans
tzolt. But his best pupil was his
andson Christoph. His work was
own all over Europe. The Armoury
llection contains one of the many
agnificent articles made by Christoph
mnitzer, remarkable for its superb
chnical execution. This is the gilded
blet in the form of an eagle, adorned
th chasing which imitates the feath-
s. It was made as a present for King
ristian IV of Denmark in 1595.

the middle of the 16th century the
mand for silverware grew and the
rcle of people who bought and com-
ssioned it expanded. Silver wine
blets and beer mugs adorned the ta-
es not only of the nobility, but also of
e middle class. The so-called
musement" goblets appeared, which
re designed to entertain guests, such
goblets in the shape of sailing ships,
m which you drank the health of
ople about to go to sea. Specimens
n be seen here.

re too you can see goblets made by
uremberg silversmiths in the Renais-
nce and Neo-Gothic styles. They are
chased with patterns which corre-
nd to their names, such as "grape",
pple" and "pineapple". Their lids
e adorned with silver bouquets of
wers and the stems are in the form of
e trunks entwined with cherubs or
all vases with handles.

the middle of the 17th century the
m of the goblet changed somewhat.
r the most part they were tall and
nder with deep bowls, narrowing in
e middle and chased with large pro-
erances. The stems were in the
pe of faceted banisters. Cartilagi-
us ornament was most widespread.

168

☐ **168. Ship goblet.** *Germany, Nuremberg,
1604–1624. Master: T. Wolf. Silver; chasing, casting, engraving, gilding. Height 48.4*

Showcase 36	WORKS OF EUROPEAN MASTERS OF THE 13TH TO EARLY 16TH CENTURIES

The Armoury collection has a few early works by West European masters which are displayed in a special showcase. They include a pyx, a vessel for the Communion host, a casket-reliquary in the form of a house with a saddleback roof and a square plate with the Crucifixion, the work of 13th-century Limoges craftsmen. The articles are made of copper and adorned with dark- and light-blue and dark-green enamel. The flowering of Limoges enamel came in the 12th and 13th centuries, but in the 14th century pride of place moved to Italy, where craftsmen began to embellish objects with transparent enamel.

The silver gilt chalice of 1330 has a smooth conical bowl and faceted stem bearing a Latin inscription in black

169

☐ **169. Chalice.** *Italy, Florence, 1330. Master: A.Arditi. Silver; gilding, enamel, carving. Height 23.5*

170

□ **170. *Casket-reliquary and pyx.*** France, Limoges, 13th century. Copper; champlevé enamel. Height of casket 15, height of pyx 8

□ **171. *Washing set: jug and bowl.*** Italy, Venice, early 16th century. Silver; gilding, enamel. Height of jug 26.5, diameter of bowl 25

enamel that reads "Andrea Arditi from Florence made me".

The hand-washing set, a jug and bowl, was the work of Venetian masters at the beginning of the 16th century. Both items are densely covered with blue, green and white enamel on which there is painting in enamel paint and gold.

The silver gilt chalice of the late 15th – early 16th century, executed in the style of Gothic architecture, with spires, Gothic arches and patterned trellises is most effective.

Grand Prince Ivan III of Moscow owned two wine vessels on display here, the 15th-century German rooster-goblet and the Hungarian goblet of King Matthias I. The body of the rooster-goblet may have originally been made from an ostrich egg shell, but was later replaced by a silver cup. Both goblets came to Russia as gifts.

172

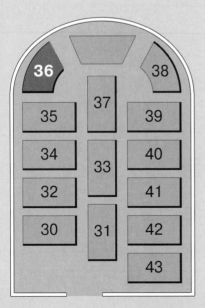

173

72. Goblet.
gary, Buda, c.
8. Silver;
sing, casting,
ing, engraving.
ght 17.9

73. Rooster
let. Germany,
15th century.
er; chasing,
ting, carving.
ght 38.5

74. Chalice.
stern Europe,
15th – early
h century. Sil-
gilding, cast-
carving.
ght 23.5

Showcase 37

COLLECTION OF ITEMS MADE OF NATURAL AND RARE MATERIALS

175

176

□ **175. Tankard.** Germany, first half of 17th century. Amber, silver; gilding, chasing, casting. Height 23

□ **176. Vase.** Germany, first half of 17th century. Amber, gold, ivory; carving, chasing. Height 32

□ **177. Goblet.** Germany, 17th century. Silver, conut; gilding, chasing, casting, engraving. Height 35

□ **178. Goblet.** Germany, 17th century. Copper, nautilus shell; chasing, casting, shell carving, gilding. Height 38.5

7   178

15th and 16th centuries were an
of geographical discoveries. New
ds appeared on the map and new
routes were opened up. Many of
trade routes from India to Europe
through Germany.
passion for sea voyages influenced
applied arts as well. Silverware was
decorated with exotic animals and
birds (camels, ostriches and parrots).
German jewellers worked not only
with silver, but also with other materials brought from eastern countries. In
their articles they combined silver with
shells of ostrich eggs, coconuts, ivory,
mother-of-pearl and glass. Note the

179

□ **179. *Drinking horn*.** *Germany, Hamburg, late 16th – early 17th century. Master: J.Mores the Elder. Ivory, silver, gems; chasing, casting, pouncing, gilding, enamel. Height 36, length 63*
□ **180. *Goblet*.** *Germany, Nuremberg; mid-16th century. Master: A.Jamnitzer. Crystal, gold, silver; chasing, casting, gilding. Height 22*

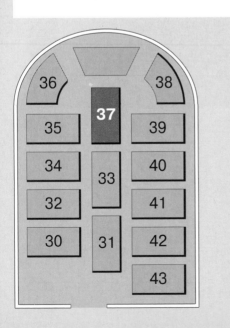

180

anciful shape of the "Nautilus" goblets made of mother-of-pearl shells set in silver. The goblets have a shining mother-of-pearl surface. To achieve his effect the master had to remove ome of the upper layers which, in a naterial as delicate as this, was no easy ask.

The goblet made by Dietrich Thor Moye is interesting. The shell cup is upported by the figure of a mermaid nd the curve of the shell is adorned with a carved pattern of fantastic birds, while Neptune crowns the silver lid. Candlesticks, tea-caddies, wine flagons and pickle bowls made of amber were brought from Pomerania and Brandenburg. The mug presented to Tsar Alexis by the Lithuanian ambassador Stanislaw Venevsky in 1648 is made of light and dark amber. The naster selected the pieces of amber with great skill. In bright sunlight they shine like pure clear honey.

The goblets made of ostrich eggshells mounted in gilded silver are most original. The three dark-brown goblets in silver-gilt mounts were carved out of coconuts by German masters in the 17th century.

German jewellers showed exceptional kill in ivory carving. The two goblets and mug displayed in the showcase have deep relief carving which reminds one of sculpture. The splendid drinking horn in a silver mount was made from an elephant tusk by the Hamburg naster Jacob Mores the Elder at the end of the 16th century. The horn is supported by the figure of a bird with outspread wings.

Here too you can see a group of objects made of rock crystal. They include an elegant crystal goblet in a gold mount. It was made in the middle of the 16th century by the well-known Nuremberg goldsmith Albrecht Jamnitzer, the brother of Wenzel Jamnitzer. Legend has it that the boyar Khvorostinin presented this goblet to False Dmitri I on

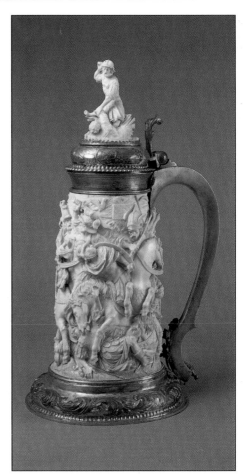

181

□ **181. *Tankard.*** *Germany, 17th century. Silver, ivory; gilding, carving, chasing, casting, engraving. Height 40*

the day of his marriage to Marina Mniscek.

<table>
<tr><td>Showcase 38</td><td>EUROPEAN JEWELLERY OF THE 16TH TO EARLY 19TH CENTURIES</td></tr>
</table>

182

□ **182. Washing set.** *Germany, Augsburg, 17th century. Master: J.H.Mannlich. Rock crystal, silver, gems; enamel. Height 43, length 64*

In showcase 38 you can see a splendid wash-jug and bowl made of rock crystal in a silver-gilt mount and decorated with enamel and precious stones (the work of the Augsburg master Johann Heinrich Mannlich). These items were brought to Russia in 1675 as presents for Tsar Alexis from the Roman Emperor Leopold I.

The showcase also contains a small collection of European jewellery of the 16th to 19th centuries. Each article here is an excellent specimen of its period.

The Medusa table decoration and the small wall altar were made at the beginning of the 17th century.

The various toilet boxes, snuffboxes, clocks and table decorations made of

□ **183. Lion and gryphon clasp.** *Western Europe, 16th century. Gold, gems; casting, enamel. Height 3.5, length 9*

83

184

□ **184. Mary On Crescent Moon pendant.** *Germany, 17th century. Gold, diamonds; casting, faceting,. Height 7.5, width 5*

□ **185. Table decoration.** *Germany, 18th century. Gold, mother-of-pearl, gems; carving. Height 18–19*

85

old and mother-of-pearl and decora-
ed with precious stones, enamelled
miniatures, porcelain and grisaille
painting date back to the middle of the
8th century.

he snuffbox with a view of St Peters-
urg on the lid was made by Swiss

masters at the beginning of the 19th
century in classical style. It is austere
in form and the colours of the enamelled miniature on the lid are fairly
subdued.

Showcase 39

THE WORK OF THE HAMBURG SILVERSMITHS

Hamburg was one of Germany's richest port towns. It was here that Russian merchants purchased gold, silver and artistic articles made of precious metals. The Hamburg jewellers were known for their unusually wide specialisation in the sphere of silver-working. The Armoury's collection of Hamburg silver consists of more than three hundred pieces and represents the work of about seventy craftsmen. In the 17th century such eminent masters as Peter Ohr, Dietrich Thor Moye, Carsten Mundt and Gregorius Lambrecht worked in this town. The Hamburg silversmith Jacob Mores the Elder was well known in the 16th century. His work is hardly to be found in the museums of Western Europe, with the exception of a jewel box in the Green

186

Vault in Dresden and the silver altar at Frederiksborg Castle in Denmark. The Armoury possesses four works by this fine jeweller. They include two huge goblets in the form of vases decorated with heads and figures cast in silver and adorned with bunches of fruit and mascarons. The third goblet by this master is somewhat smaller, but similar in form and ornament to the preceding ones. The fourth item can

☐ **186. Goblet.** *Germany, Hamburg, c. 1600. Master: J.Mores the Elder. Silver; gilding, chasing, casting, engraving. Height 58*

☐ **187. Fumigator.** *Germany, Hamburg, c. 1610. Master: D.Utermarke. Silver; gilding, chasing, casting, engraving. Height 54*

186 *A Guide*   THE ARMOURY

be seen in showcase 37, the drinking horn carved from an elephant's tusk and mounted in silver.

Jacob Mores the Elder did a great deal of work for the Danish court. His activity helped to raise the skill of the Hamburg goldsmiths and attract many esteemed orders from the royal courts of Denmark and Sweden.

These goblets were also made for the royal treasury, but it was soon to lose them. After his defeat in the Thirty Years War, King Christian IV of Denmark pawned many valuables from his treasury and since he did not have the money to redeem them in time, they were put up for sale in Archangel, where they were acquired for the Russian royal court in 1628.

The Armoury also possesses works by other famous Hamburg masters. Some candlesticks, pickle bowls and globes of the earth and the heavens made by him were brought to Russia as ambassadorial gifts from Sweden and are on display in showcase 33.

The two silver fumigators in this showcase were made in the first quarter of the 17th century by Dirich Utermarke

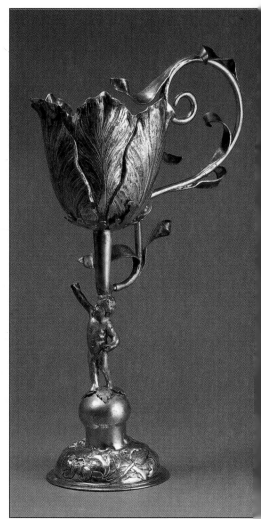

188

☐ **188. Goblet.** *Germany, Hamburg, 17th century. Silver; gilding, chasing, casting, engraving. Height 35.5, diameter 15.5*
☐ **189. Dish.** *Germany, Hamburg, 17th century. Silver; chasing, engraving, gilding. Diameter 38*

189

d Flor Robin II, contemporaries of cob Mores the Elder. They belonged Tsar Michael Romanov and were pt in his apartments.

aracteristic features of Hamburg ar- les are high-relief chasing, the use of t engraving and the development of corative sculpture. From the 1650s mburg art adopted the so-called

"floral fashion". Examples of this are the vase with a tulip-shaped bowl and the dish chased with floral ornament. The sumptuous royal receptions and the custom of awarding silver articles for various services, namely, to ambassa- dors for carrying out diplomatic mis- sions, to military men for successful campaigns and to "customs and tavern heads" for replenishing the state coffers, required a vast amount of silverware. The Moscow government gave foreign masters special commissions for items of silver. And the objects produced by these commissions had a typically Russian form. This explains why we find loving-cups among the goblets, wash-jugs and dishes.

In the 17th century silver plate began to appear in the homes of boyars, courtiers and merchants. True, it was used only on very special occasions and kept on special stands as precious objects brought from abroad or awarded for loyal service. In Russia, as in the West, the goblet was the object most commonly awarded. On his accession to the throne Tsar Alexis received more than two hundred silver goblets from boyars, merchants, monasteries and settlements.

Later Tsar Alexis and his son Alexis were presented by the boyar B.Morozov with two silver goblets (on open display) about two metres high, weighing 16 kilograms each. They were the work of the German master Hans Frünsfeldt.

Open display.
Barodue silver ornaments of palace interiors

<table>
<tr><td>

Showcase 40

</td><td>

AUGSBURG SILVER
OF THE AGE OF BAROQUE –
17TH TO EARLY 18TH CENTURIES

</td></tr>
</table>

The Armoury possesses the world's largest collection of works by Augsburg silversmiths. It consists of more than four hundred magnificent items from the 16th to the early 18th century. Augsburg flourished thanks to its favourable geographical position. It was situated on trade routes running from the south to the north. Between 1525 and 1575 there were about a hundred gold- and silversmiths working here. Their articles were well known and in great demand. The goblets, figured wash-jugs, fireplace decorations and wine vessels of the most varied forms show a high technique of execution, fine ornament and beautiful proportions.

Like Nuremberg, Augsburg was famous for its family traditions. Jewellery-

190

□ **190. Candlestick vase.** *Germany, Augsburg, second half of 17th century. Master: A. Drentwett II. Silver; chasing, casting, carving, gilding. Height 48*

king skills were passed down from
eration to generation here. For two
ndred and fifty years the artists and
ersmiths of the Drentwett family
rked in the town. Their articles were
own in many countries. The parlia-
nt in Stockholm, for example, con-
is a silver throne made for Queen
ristina by Abraham Drentwett I.
e Armoury possesses silverware
de by several members of this fami-
Abraham Drentwett II made two
ndlesticks in the form of vases of
vers, which were sent from Vienna
1684 with other ambassadorial gifts.
te the goblet in the form of Diana
a deer, which was designed to en-
ain guests at table. The Augsburg
sters had a weakness for figured ves-
. The deer's head served as the lid.
e wine was poured into the body.
d in the base of the goblet was a
ck mechanism which set the deer's
ly in motion. The guest in whose di-
tion the deer turned had the right to
pty the goblet.
e sumptuousness of palaces and pal-
ceremonies led to the appearance
massive silver tableware, buckets,
red wash-jugs, vases, mugs and
d decorations in baroque style.
ese objects show a pronounced dec-
tive element. Foliate motifs and dise variations on the cartilaginous
ament typical of baroque predomi-
ed.
example of this is the silver plate
h a scene of Turkish prisoners be-
e the Emperor Leopold I after the
tory of the Austro-Polish army over
Turks at Vienna in the autumn of
3. The plate was made by Lorenz
er II.
e water vessel by the Augsburg gold-
th David Schwestermüller in the
n of King Charles I of England on
rancing horse is most original.
hwestermüller created a whole series
able ornaments and vessels depict-
European monarchs.

191

192

☐ **191. Diana amusement goblet.** Germany,
Augsburg, 1610–1620. Master: J.Fries. Silver; gilding, chasing, casting, engraving. Height 44
☐ **192. Dish.** Germany, Augsburg, second half of
17th century. Master: L.Biller II. Silver; chasing,
casting, pouncing, gilding. Oval 78×98

☐ **193. *Vessel depicting King Charles I on horseback.*** *Germany, Augsburg, first half of 17th century. Master: D.Schwestermüller. Silver; gilding, casting, engraving. Height 44.5*

193

194

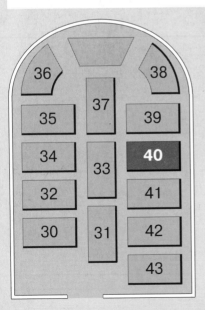

The Augsburg craftsmen were famed for the silver furniture which they made for palace apartments. On open display you can see two large mirrors in silver frames by Abraham Drentwett II and silver tables made at the beginning of the 18th century by Johann Engelbrent. The mirror and tables are decorated with splendid chasing and casting in baroque and Regency style.

194. *Table
untain.* *Germa-
, Augsburg, c.
40–1645. Mas-
: G.B.Wainold l.
ver; gilding,
sting. Height
.7, diameter
.3

195. *Mirror in
ver frame.
rmany, Augs-
rg, 1690. Mas-
: A Drentwett ll.
ver; chasing,
sting. Height
0, width 200*

195

<table>
<tr><td>

Showcase 41

</td><td>

THE ART OF THE FRENCH SILVERSMITHS FROM THE 17TH TO EARLY 18TH CENTURIES

</td></tr>
</table>

At the beginning of the 18th century in Western Europe pride of place moved from German to French master jewellers. Two showcases in this room (41 and 42) contain gold and silver articles by French craftsmen.

Diplomatic and trading relations between Russia and France existed already in the 16th century, but there was no custom of presenting ambassadorial gifts in France. So nearly all the objects in these showcases were commissioned.

Very few pieces of French silver made before the 18th century have survived, because at the end of the 17th century and in the first half of the 18th several royal edicts were issued on melting down gold- and silverware for coinage to replenish the royal coffers which

196

□ **196. Wash jug.** *France, Paris, first half of 17th century. Silver; chasing, casting, pouncing, gilding. Diameter 45*

☐ **197. Dish.**
*France, Paris, first
half of 17th century. Silver; chasing, casting,
pouncing, gilding.
Diameter 45*

197

d been emptied by wars and the extravagance of the court. Thus many orks of art by eminent French craftsen were lost, which would otherwise ve rightfully won a place in the easury of world art.

e early specimens of 17th-century rench jewellery on display here inude a silver gilt plate and wash-jug ought to Russian in 1664 as a diplotic gift for Tsar Alexis from King harles II of England. The wash-jug is corated with chased muses and the ate with a scene of the besieged city Torquato Tasso's "Jerusalem Delivered".

Eighteenth-century France dictated the fashions in Europe. Anxious not to be outdone by their West-European "brothers", Russian monarchs commissioned the best French jewellers to make them gold toilet sets, boxes, snuffboxes (at that time it was fashionable for women as well as men to take snuff) and services.

Noteworthy among the early 18th-century articles is the soup bowl by the master Antoine de Saint-Nicholas. It is adorned with engraved ornament on a pounced background. Bowls of this sort could be used to serve clear soup instead of morning coffee.

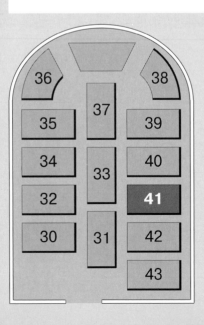

□ **198. Soup bowl from Orl** **service.** Franc Paris, 1770–17 Master: J.N.Roettiers. ver; chasing, casting, pounc ing. Height 33

198

Many of the objects displayed in this showcase formed part of the services commissioned by Catherine the Great in the 1770s for the thirty new administrative centres of Russia. Here you can see items from the Moscow, Nizhny Novgorod, Kazan and Yekaterinoslav services. The services were intended for official receptions. The leading French master Robert Joseph Auguste, who signed his articles with the words "Auguste – gold- and silver-smith to the King in Paris", took part in making them.

In 1770 Catherine the Great commissioned a silver dinner service in France which she later presented to her favourite Grigory Orlov. More than two tons of silver went into it. The service

99

☐ **199. Bouillon bowl.** *France, Paris, first half of 18th century. Master: A.de Saint-Nicolas. Silver; gilding, chasing. Diameter 25*

onsisted of more than three thousand eces and was intended for forty per- ons.

he commission went to Jean Roet- ers and his son. However, the large umber of items made it impossible for em to complete the service on their wn, and they were assisted by Edme- ierre Balzac, Louis Lehendrick, Paul harvel and other masters. The artistic pervisor was the famous French ulptor Falconet, author of the statue Peter the Great in St Petersburg. small part of this service has survived d is on display in the Armoury and e State Hermitage. In the showcase here you can see soup tureens, wine slides, plates, candlesticks and shell-like dishes for butter.

The Orlov service is so magnificent that in 1881 a copy of it was made for the Victoria and Albert Museum in London.

Showcase 42   FRENCH EMPIRE SILVER

200

The beginning of the 19th century witnessed a remarkable flowering of the applied arts in France, caused by the luxury of Napoleon's court. Paris jewellers received numerous commissions from the emperor himself.

The Armoury possesses several items by Jean-Baptiste Odiot, whose works adorned the palaces of Napoleon. Objects made by this master were valued highly in Russia and purchased in large quantities. Services, vases and soup tureens by Odiot can be found in the Hermitage and the Armoury.

The master worked in the so-called Empire style, which is characterised by dense gilding, a perfectly polished surface and a matt applied ornament of classical figures, vases, wreaths and lyres.

□ **200. Tea and coffee service.** France, Paris, early 19th century. Coffee pot, teapot, milk jug – J.-B.C.Odiot. Spoons – F.D.Naudin. Cups and saucers – Denuel and Neppel manufactory. Silver, mother-of-pearl, porcelain; casting, stamping, rolling, gilding, glazing. Height of coffee pot 25.5, teapot 18, milk jug 19, cups 13.5, length of tongs 14.5, spoon 15, tray 57, width of tray 35, diameter of saucers 14

□ **201. Vase.** France, Paris, early 19th century. Master: M.G.Biennais. Silver; stamping, chasing, pouncing, gilding. Height 72

201

In the showcase you can see a tea service for two made in 1825 by Odiot and Naudin. The service consists of cups, a milk jug and two teapots with mother-of-pearl handles. The cups and saucers in this service are made of china, although the shining surface gives the impression that they are of metal. The fine metal-chaser Martin Guillaume Biennais also worked in the Empire style. The showcase contains a silver gilt vase by him. It was presented by the city magistrate to the commander of the Russian corps in Paris, Count M.S.Vorontsov, in 1819.

The vase is in the form of a Greek crater and is decorated with compositions of weapons, armour, winged female figures symbolising victory, and also the chased coat-of-arms of the Vorontsovs.

Showcase 43   THE OLYMPIC SERVICE

In the 18th century silver, the main material used for making services, was replaced by porcelain. Until then the secret of making porcelain was not known in Europe and was closely guarded by the Chinese masters who possessed it.

In the first half of 18th century a method of making porcelain was discovered in three European countries. In Russia it was invented by D.I.Vinogradov, then perfected by M.V.Lomonosov. St Petersburg became the centre of porcelain manufacturing. In Germany the centre was Meissen and in France it was Sèvres, a small town then not far from Paris and now one of its suburbs. The Sèvres manufactory was a very large porcelain enterprise. One of the main lines of its activity right from its founding in the middle of the 18th century was the creation of magnificent services for diplomatic gifts.

The showcase contains a porcelain dessert service made at the Sèvres manufactory in 1803–1806 and intended for the personal use of Emperor Napoleon. This service adorned the banquet table at the Tuileries on the occasion of the marriage of the Princess of Württemberg to Napoleon's brother, Jérome Bonaparte. It consists of 140 pieces and is called the Olympic service, because the subjects for the designs are taken from Greek mythology. It is interesting that no design or subject is repeated on the items. In most cases the originals for the painting were works of art from various countries and schools. The service was painted by the artists Adam, Jacoteau, Le Grand, Perrenaux, Renault and Tiboux and ornamented by Miquot and Livet the Elder.

In 1807 Napoleon presented the service to Alexander I to commemorate the Peace of Tilsit.

CLOCKS BY DAVID ROENTGEN

This room contains grandfather clocks by the famous cabinet-maker David Roentgen (1743–1807). A German by birth, he inherited his father's workshop in the town of Neuwied, which employed more than a hundred joiners, bronze-smiths, carvers and other craftsmen, became a member of the Paris guild of cabinet-makers in 1770 and was a supplier to Louis XVI and Marie Antoinette. He visited St Petersburg seven times and on each occasion

202

□ **202–204.**
Plates from Ol-
ympic service.
France, Sèvres,
early 19th centu-
ry. Porcelain;
painting, gilding.
Diameter 23.4

03

204

atherine the Great purchased many
ems from him.
avid Roentgen created his own style
f furniture. From the 1770s his work
as distinguished by rectangular out-
nes and symmetrical, classical forms.
lis decorative elements were bor-
owed from Greek and Roman art:
ams, meanders, pearl-oysters, eagles,
olphins and sheep heads.

Roentgen liked designing furniture
with secrets (cabinets, writing desks
and secretaires) and embellishing it
with chasing, gilded bronze and inlay.
The clock case is made of mahogany
and bronze in classical style. The clock
mechanism is the work of 18th-century
German craftsmen.

GROUND FLOOR *(Continued)*

| ROOM 6 | PRECIOUS FABRICS, PICTORIAL AND ORNAMENTAL EMBROIDERY OF THE 14TH TO 18TH CENTURIES, RUSSIAN SECULAR DRESS IN OF THE 16TH TO EARLY 20TH CENTURY |

In the 14th century Moscow became a major political, religious and cultural centre with strong diplomatic and trading relations with East and West. Many of the exhibits in this room testify to the enhanced importance of the Moscow principality.

Foreign merchants and embassies with various missions brought expensive gifts for the princes of Moscow. And among these "offerings" it was not uncommon to find precious fabrics – satin, damask, axamite and velvet from Byzantium, Persia, Turkey, Spain, France and Italy.

ne "wares from overseas" were first
xamined and selected by the prince's
ater the tsar's) representatives, and
nly after that were the fabrics sold.
hey were very expensive and could be
afforded only by boyars and the higher
clergy, who made sumptuous garments
from them adorned with pearls and
precious stones.

a mediaeval Russia dress was a most
nportant feature in the overall deco-
tive appearance of the monarch and
e clergy. The sumptuous robes of the
Moscow princes, tsars and representa-
ves of the church were made with a
efinite political aim in mind. And this
aim, as the reports and accounts of
foreign visitors who describe the richness of the Russian court show, was almost always achieved.

In the variety of the fabrics and their
excellent state of preservation this collection is one of the finest in the world.

Showcase 44

RUSSIAN SECULAR DRESS IN THE 16TH AND 17TH CENTURIES

The specimens of secular dress of the 16th and 17th centuries in the Armoury collection are extremely rare. They illustrate the general features characteristic of Russian national costume and, in addition, are precisely dated and connected with specific historical figures. There were many forms of dress in mediaeval Russia, as can be seen from early documents.

Dress always expresses certain criteria of beauty which exist in this or that nation. The ideal of beauty in Old Russia was a stately figure, a proud bearing and a smooth gait. Consequently clothing was long and loose-fitting. It created a majestic visual image and did not accentuate the form of the body. The style of most clothing of the pre-Petrine age (with the exception of courtiers' and

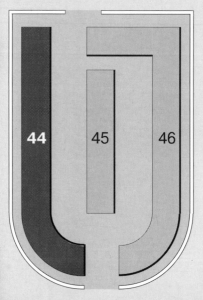

officials' dress) was the same for all sections of the population.

A boyar's dress differed from that of a common man mainly in the quality of the fabric, the decorations and the number of items worn. The common people wore clothes made of linen, coarse coloured cotton and homespun wool. The clothes of the rich were made of imported precious fabrics.

The earliest item of clothing in the collection is Metropolitan Philip's fur coat, a unique specimen of 16th-century Russian popular dress. It is made of homespun dark-brown wool and lined with sheepskin. The metropolitan wore this coat during his exile at the Otroch-Assumption monastery in Tver.

Fur coats were very common in Russia and were worn by all sections of the population. The peasants made them with a lining of sheepskin or hare fur, the boyars and clergy with a lining of sable, marten or white fox. The collar and cuffs were of fur. With the fur coat they wore tall straight hats made from the neck fur of the marten, sable or fox.

A rare item of clothing, of which only one has survived, is the *nalatnik* which was worn over ceremonial armour. In cut it resembles a jacket open at the sides with short sleeves. The specimen on display is made of red satin densely covered with gold embroidery. It belonged to Tsar Michael Romanov.

The main type of male upper garment in mediaeval Russia was the *zipun*, which was worn over a long shirt. It was unfastened with the edges just meeting. The long narrow sleeves were gathered at the wrist with hooks. A smallish

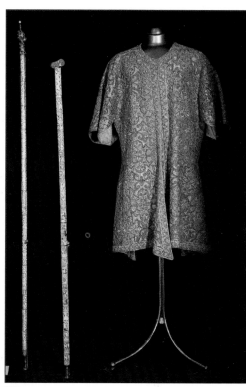

☐ **205. Nalat-
nik.** *Satin, gold
thread, embroi-
dery. Length 97.5,
width of hem 121*

und collar was attached on top. The
zipun was encircled at the waist several
times by an oriental belt. In the showcase you can see the domestic *zipun* of
Peter the Great, made of green satin
and quilted lengthwise with strips of
padding.

The largest group of garments on display are the kaftans, a long-skirted coat
which was worn over the *zipun*. The
earliest specimen is a 16th-century oriental kaftan. It is made of pale blue
Persian satin. The pattern, woven in silk
and gold, shows a man fighting a dragon.
The cut oriental kaftans differed little from
those accepted in Russia and were often
worn there without any alterations.

The style of Peter the Great's kaftan of
dark green cloth is reminiscent of a folk

poddyovka, (a light, tight-fitting coat).
This type of kaftan was very widespread
in Russia. The "figured kaftans", so-
called because they were close-fitting,
were made of more expensive fabrics.
The nobility usually wore them at
home. They were long and unbuttoned,
with the waist slightly gathered at the
back and broad short sleeves, from
which the sleeves of the *zipun* protrud-
ed, fastened at the wrist by cuffs embroidered with pearls and precious
stones.

In the showcase you can see three figured kaftans belonging to Peter the
Great which were made at the end of
the 17th century in the Kremlin workshop. They are similar in cut, adorned
with silver-gilt lace and made of white

watered and pinkish, dark red silk and
pale blue wool.

On ordinary days the tsar's clothing was
the same as that of his boyars, but on official occasions, such as coronations
and receptions for foreign ambassadors,
the royal attire was extremely sumptuous. For such occasions there was a special robe called a *platno*, which only the
tsar was allowed to wear. It was a long,
unfastened garment, very flared at the
bottom, with broad short sleeves. The
platno was made of the most expensive
imported fabrics, brocade, axamite and
altabas.

The sides, cuffs and hem were trimmed
with gold or silver lace, precious stones
and pearls. A broad round collar (humeral) decorated with small icons and
precious stones was worn on top and a
pectoral cross or gold chain consisting
of double-headed eagles was put on over
the humeral.

In the centre of the showcase is a *platno*
made of Venetian axamite for Peter the
Great in 1691. The decorations on the
platno have not survived. Old invento-
ries say that it was trimmed with sable

206

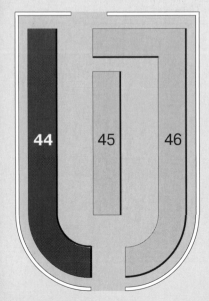

and had gold buttons with emeralds.

Two kaftans belonging to Peter the
Great have an unusual cut. Contact
with the countries of the West and East
naturally influenced the everyday life
and dress of the Russians. Peter was the
first to wear kaftans with a "foreign"
cut. The kaftan of red Dutch cloth (on
the left) was made in April 1690. It is
perforated at the waist, the bodice is
close-fitting and the lower flaps consist
of pieces of cloth sewn together and
gathered. The sleeves, wide and sumptuous at the top, narrow from the elbow
to the wrist, ending in a broad flair. The

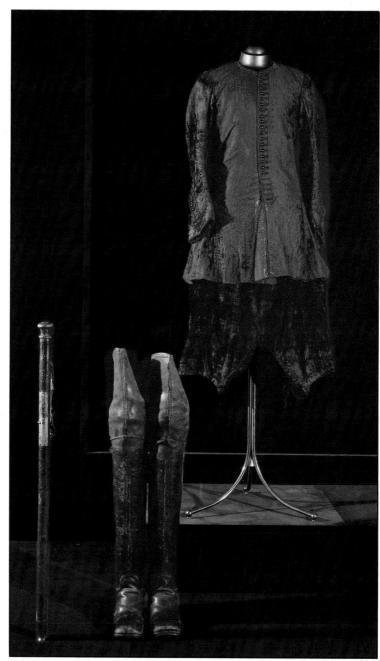

206. *Riding*
ftan (terlik).
scow Kremlin
rkshops, sec-
d half of 17th
ntury. Velvet;
pliqué work.
ngth 124, width
em 140
207. *Kaftan,*
kboots,
ne.
onged to Tsar
er the Great

chest is decorated with appliqué work of silver cord with tassels.

The other kaftan, made of black velvet of the Dutch type, consists of a close-fitting jacket and short, wide trousers. It was very suitable for working in. Peter is thought to have worn it when he worked in the shipyards in Holland, where he studied shipbuilding.

A statesman, military and naval commander and diplomat, Peter the Great learned several trades: he was also a joiner, carpenter and bootmaker. The jackboots on display here were actually made by the emperor himself. They could be worn over fur boots. The foot section is 29.5 cm long and the top 90 cm high. Judging by the inscription on it which says: "From the hands of the Transformer and made by his own hand" the applewood cane was also made by Peter.

In the 17th century the nobility began to wear another type of ceremonial upper garment, the *ferezeya*. It was made of precious fabrics, such as brocade, velvet and fine wool. The *ferezeya* was lined with fur and occasionally embroidered with pearls and precious stones. It was a long, straight garment worn over the shoulders and fastened at the neck only by a tasselled cord or a stud. The armholes were open in front and you could put your arms through them. The sleeves were very long, down to the ground, and were tossed back and tied behind the back. The Russian expression "to work letting your sleeves down" would appear to be connected with this rather awkward garment.

The *ferezeya* on the left in the showcase was made of white woollen fabric in the second half of the 17th century. It is thought to have belonged to Tsar Alexis. Unfortunately it gives one an idea only of the cut of the *ferezeya* as none of the decorations have survived.

The headwear of a high-born Russian woman consisted of a kind of tiara, or *kokoshnik* decorated with silver-gilt lace, enamel and pearls. Braided strings of pearls with precious stones hung from the temples to the shoulders on gold chains or rings. The neck was adorned by necklaces in the form of pearls sewn onto material or threaded. Russian women were also very fond of metal necklaces with precious stones.

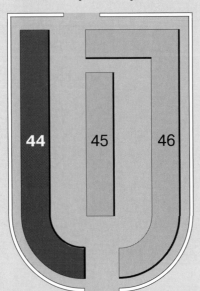

208

☐ **208. Boot.**
Russia, second half of 17th century. Velvet, leather, pearls. Height 5[ ], length of foot 2[ ]

□ **209.** *Platno with humeral.* Moscow Kremlin
Workshops, late 17th century. Axamite – Venice,
17th century. Gold lace – Western Europe, 17th
century. Length 166.5, length of sleeve 52, width of
hem 380. Belonged to Tsar Peter the Great

Earrings with two or three pendants were a favourite ornament in Old Russia. Earrings and signet rings were made of gold and silver and adorned with very fine filigree, enamel, niello and tiny drops of metal known as seeds of gold. The precious stones were not cut, only polished slightly to bring out their natural beauty.

Special significance was attached to precious stones in Old Russia. The emerald, for example, was regarded as the stone of wisdom, the sapphire "discloses treachery and drives away fear", and the ruby "cures the heart and mind". Warriors decorated their weapons with diamonds in the belief that this would protect them.

Buttons were an important feature of dress decoration: gold buttons with enamel and diamonds or coral; silver ones the size of a hen's egg with relief designs and different coloured enamel for heavy fur coats; and small ones no bigger than a pea, in the shape of a tiny ball or acorn for kaftans, zipuns, padded jackets and other items of dress, both male and female. Buttons sometimes cost more than the garment itself.

For example, Peter the Great's *platno* made in 1722 was valued at 70 roubles and the buttons on it at 606 roubles.

An essential part of female dress was the *shirinka* headscarf, which was made according to the width (*shirina*) of the material. The showcase contains several specimens made of 17th-century Italian taffeta and skilfully trimmed by Russian needlewomen with braided gold lace and seed pearls. It was the custom for a Russian bride-to-be to present her fiancé with several headscarves of this kind.

Footwear in old Russia was made of brightly coloured leather, brocade and velvet. Up to the 16th century it had a soft sole, but in the 17th century women's boots acquired heels, sometimes as much as 11 cm high. The showcase contains a pair of 17th-century woman's boots made of velvet embroidered with pearls.

44	**45**	**46**

210

□ **210. *Volosnik.*** Moscow Kremlin Workshops, 16th–17th cent. Gold and silver thread, satin, wire silk, braiding, embroidery. Height 16.3, circumference 56.2

1

□ **211. Mirror.** *Istanbul, first quarter of 17th century. Gold, gems, jade, mirror; casting, chasing, carving, engraving. Diameter 19.3, length 42*

212

□ **212. Button.** *Russia, 17th century. Gold; enamel. Diameter 2.6, length 3.5*

213

□ **213. Button.** *Russia, 17th century. Gold; enamel. Diameter 2.8, length 5.1*

Showcase 45

RUSSIAN SECULAR DRESS IN THE 18TH AND 19TH CENTURIES

Until the beginning of the 18th century Russians wore national costume. In 1700–1701 Peter the Great issued an edict to replace traditional Russian dress, which was long and hard to work in, by fashionable European clothing. Apart from the peasants and clergy, all the urban male population had to shave off their beards and wear curled wigs. These reforms encountered fierce opposition, particularly from the boyars. True, the tsar eventually gave way to those who adamantly refused to part with their beards. But this step was not a disinterested one. Every man who chose to keep his "male pride and joy" had to pay a tax to the exchequer for the right to do so. Special copper coins were even issued bearing a beard and moustache with the inscription "Money paid".

Long garments were replaced by the short kaftan, camisole and narrow knee-length breeches. The costume also included a shirt with a splendid lace jabot and cuffs, long silk hose, high-heeled shoes and a wig with long curled hair.

The kaftans of Tsar Peter II were made in the French fashion at the beginning of the 18th century. He died early, at the age of fifteen, from smallpox. His costumes were not touched for a long time, evidently for fear of infection, and consequently his rich wardrobe has survived intact. The kaftans are made of velvet, brocade and wool.

Camisoles were of lighter materials, rep and light brocade. The shoulders

ere slightly tapered and canvas was
serted in the lower folds to widen the
irt of the kaftan slightly. The gar-

ment was richly trimmed with gold and
silver lace.

214

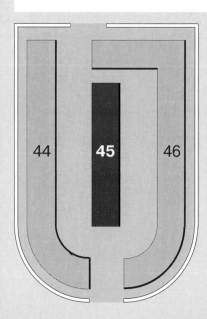

Women found it particularly hard to get used to the new fashions. They had to give up their sarafans and sleeveless jackets which concealed the forms of the body and replace them by dresses with very low necklines and short sleeves. It was not easy to overcome this "psychological barrier". The traditional bonnets under which women hid their hair were also "abolished", and the hair was curled into ringlets and arranged in extravagant coiffures. Having previously led a secluded life at home, women now received the right to attend various celebrations, parades and so-called assemblies (a new type of meeting introduced by Peter the Great with food and dancing, where business could also be transacted).

☐ **214. Coronation dress.** *Russia, 1724. Silk; silver embroidery, weaving. Belonged to Empress Catherine I*

☐ **215. Coronation dress.** *Russia, 1730. Brocade, silk, gold lace, braid; embroidery, weaving. Belonged to Empress Anne*

216

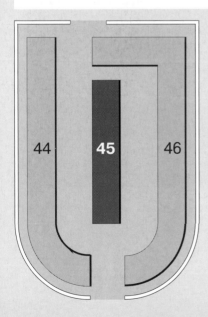

□ **216. Coron** **tion dress.** *Ru* *sia, 1742. Silve* *brocade, silk,* *gold lace; weav* *ing, embroidery* *Belonged to Er* *press Elizabeth*
□ **217. Wed-** **ding dress.** *R* *sia, 1745. Silve* *brocade, silk; s* *embroidery.* *Belonged to* *Grand Duchess* *Catherine. (late* *Empress Cathe* *ine the Great)*

At first women were strongly opposed to Peter's reforms concerning everyday life, but they soon realised the advantages of the innovations and gave them active support.

The two coronation dresses on display which belonged to the Russian empresses Catherine I and Anne were made in the style fashionable in Europe at the beginning of the 18th century. The dresses have a close-fitting bodice, which was typical of female dress throughout the whole of the 18th century, a low-cut neckline, very small short sleeves and a wide bell-shaped skirt. In order to produce this bell shape, whalebone hoops were sewn into the underskirt. This type of skirt remained in fashion until the 1760s and was known as a pannier skirt.

44 **45** 46

blue masked-ball dress of the
)s in the showcase belonged to
ierine I. It consists of a male-cut
an embroidered with silk and a
isole with a broad silver fringe.
re is also a matching pair of silver-
roidered shoes.

Empress Anne's coronation dress is
made of pink brocade. The original
colour has survived in the folds only.
The bodice ends in a hard narrow
point. The train is lighter than in the
1720s. Note the handmade silver-gilt
lace covering the skirt.

In the middle of the 18th century the cut of clothes followed the extravagant lines of rococo, the predominant style of the day. The fashion was for narrow shoulders, a tiny waist and a skirt that flared out on whalebone farthingales. The farthingales were up to 1.5 metres wide and the hems as much as five metres in circumference. There are three dresses with farthingales in the showcase.

The coronation dress of Empress Elizabeth made in 1742 of silver brocade is sleeveless, with a low neckline and lace trimming. The handmade silver lace mantle is most sumptuous. It is 5.18 metres long and weighs five kilograms.

Elizabeth and her court spent the time in endless amusements, such as masked balls, hunting parties and picnics. The empress herself spent vast sums on her wardrobe. The historian V.O.Klyuchevsky writes: "...after her death she left 15,000 dresses, two trunks full of stockings and ... heaps of unpaid bills."

The light wedding dress (1745) in which Catherine the Great was married is made of silver brocade and embroidered in silver thread. Here too is her coronation dress (1762) embroidered in gold with double-headed eagles.

Catherine the Great's court was no less sumptuous than that of her predecessor. The dresses of the court ladies shone with gold and silver lace and precious stones. The costumes, hats and sword hilts of the court dandies were studded with diamonds and other valuables. The extravagance of the court reached such proportions that Catherine was forced to issue an edict regulating ceremonial and court dress. One of the points in the edict specified that gold and silver lace on kaftans should not be more than nine centimetres wide.

At the end of the 18th century the interest in classicism led to a sudden change in fashion. Dresses were now high-waisted with a straight skirt modelled on the Greek chiton and tunic. Hair styles changed as well. Extravagant coiffures were replaced by free-flowing locks and a Grecian knot.

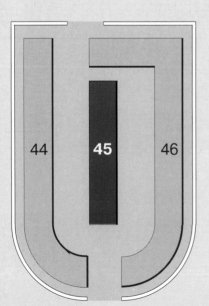

218

□ **218. Kaftans and camisoles.** *France, 1727–
1730. Brocade, silk, velvet; gold embroidery, appliqué work.
Belonged to Emperor Peter II*

219

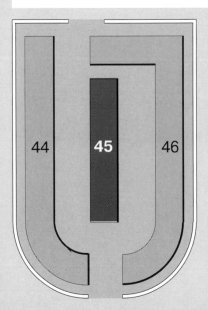

☐ **219. Fan.** *St Petersburg, House of Fabergé, 1899–1908. Master: H.Wigström. Gold, silver, diamonds, chrysolites, mother-of-pearl, foil, paper; chasing, enamel, guilloche, carving, water colour. Length 23*
☐ **220. Coronation dress.** *Russia, 1762. Brocade; decorative embroidery on appliqué work lace.*
Belonged to Empress Catherine the Great

Ceremonial dress of the early 19th century reflected the renewed interest in history and national traditions. Official dresses now had long sleeves resembling those in the 17th century. They were still made of silver brocade, which was the privilege of the imperial family only, on heavy silk or satin. **T**he coronation dresses of 1856 and 1896 observe the rules of official dress. The renewal of interest in Old Russia affected the ornament as well. The coronation dress (1896) of Tsarina Alexandra Fyodorovna is embroidered with silver faceted thread and thousands of small pearls. From the 18th century the official ceremonial dress of the emperor was the uniform of the Preobrazhensky Life Guards. A coro-

☐ **221.** *Coronation dress. Russia, 1825. Brocade, silver thread; wire-work, embroidery.*
Belonged to Empress Alexandra Fyodorovna, the wife of Nicholas I

221

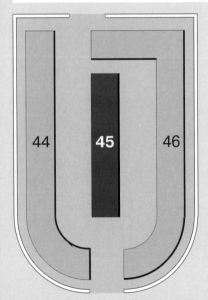

nation mantle of gold or silver gilt brocade trimmed with ermine was an essential part of the coronation attire. Here you can see the coronation mantle of 1896.

The items on display on the elegant tables in the showcase testify to the variety of fashionable accessories which added to the sumptuousness of ceremonial attire in the 18th and 19th centuries, such as fans, lorgnettes, snuffboxes, watches, swords, canes, etc.

Fans were known in Russia in the 17th century, but became far more wide-

2

□ **222.** *Coronation dress.* Russia, 1856. Brocade, silver thread; wire-work, embroidery.
Belonged to Empress Maria Alexandrovna, the wife
of Alexander II

spread in the 18th. They were used by ladies in the privileged classes outside and at theatres and balls. Fans were carried on a band round the wrist of the right hand.

In the 18th century painted silk fans usually with a wooden, tortoiseshell or mother-of-pearl frame were very fashionable. They were sometimes made of paper instead of silk. A fan of this kind is on display in the showcase. On the paper are scenes from peasant life (the work of the French artist Boucher). On the paper of another fan, with a frame of mother-of-pearl and ivory, is a picture of Catherine the Great attending the partition of Poland. There is also a fan made in Russia at the end of the 18th century with a family portrait of the Golitsyn princes.

The fashion for taking snuff produced all manner of snuffboxes made of gold, mother-of-pearl, crystal and other materials. Gold snuffboxes studded with precious stones and bearing a portrait of the emperor or empress were often presented to favourites.

The ceremonial court dress for men included swords, canes and daggers.

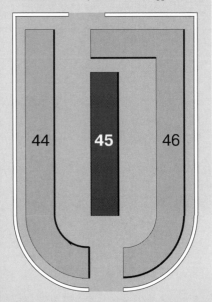

Coronation uniform of Emperor Nicholas II and coronation dress of Empress Alexandra Fyodorovna
□ **223. Coronation mantle.** *Russia, 1896. Brocade, silk, fur, satin ribbon, gold thread; embroidery. Length 450.*
Belonged to Empress Alexandra Fyodorovna, the wife of Nicholas II

The hilt of the court dagger on display here is decorated with about 700 diamonds, and the handle of the pearwood cane with 490 diamonds and emeralds. Dandies used to wear lots of "musical watches" usually on a chain or a lace which was often woven from the hair of the beloved.

☐ **224. Masked ball costume.** *Moscow, 1903. Studs, buttons – Constantinople, second half of 17th century. Brocade, velvet, silk, satin, gold, gems, pearls; weaving, embroidery, chasing, enamel, braiding, threading.*
Belonged to Emperor Nicholas II

44   **45**   46

224

☐ **225. *Coronation dress.*** *Russia, 1896. Brocade, silk, silver thread; pearls, lace; embroidery,
threading.*
*Belonged to Empress Alexandra Fyodorovna, the
wife of Nicholas II*

Showcase 46	PRECIOUS FABRICS FROM BYZANTIUM, PERSIA AND TURKEY OF THE 14TH TO 17TH CENTURIES

The earliest fabrics in the Armoury collection are Byzantine. They were brought to Russia by merchants and annual embassies. Byzantine cross-patterned satins were particularly prized in Russia. They were used to make robes for the higher clergy. On the right in the showcase you can see a 1322 saccos (a vestment worn by a bishop) of light-blue satin with vertical gold stripes and crosses in circles. It belonged to the first metropolitan of Moscow, Peter. (In 1325 Metropolitan Peter moved from Vladimir to Moscow, an event of great importance for the enhancement of the principality. Moscow thus became the country's religious as well as political centre.)

Note the saccos, epitrachelion (stole) and cuffs of Metropolitan Alexis (1348–1378), an eminent churchman of Muscovite Russia. Here the Byzantine fabric serves merely as a background for the gold crosses embroidered on it. Between the crosses are small decorative plates of 13th-century Russian cloisonné enamel.

The "large" saccos of Metropolitan Photius and "small" one, which may also have belonged to him, are made of Byzantine fabric. The "small" saccos is embroidered with the figure of Metropolitan Peter. And the "large" saccos is embroidered in coloured silks, gold and silver with portraits of Grand Prince Vassily of Moscow, his wife Sofia Witowna, their daughter Anna and her husband (the future Emperor John Palaeologus of Byzantium) and also a por-

trait of Photius himself. All the portraits are framed with pearls.

The portrait of a Russian prince together with the emperor of Byzantium testifies to the growing importance of the Moscow state. The Byzantine fabrics in the Armoury collection are extremely valuable. The only other museums where such fabrics can be found are in Athens and London. A large

number are also in private collections and churches.

The saccos of Metropolitan Simon (1496–1519) is made of dark-red satin. The collar and cuffs are adorned with chased silver plates by Russian craftsmen.

In the 16th and 17th centuries permanent trading relations were set up between the Russian state and both Persia and Turkey. From the Orient came mostly silk fabrics, in the quality and quantity of which the treasury of the Moscow tsars was unequalled.

The Persian fabrics in the Armoury collection date back to the 17th century, a period which saw the flowering of Persian weaving in the towns of Kashan, Isfahan, Tabriz and Resht. Persian satin, velvet, taffeta, damask and brocade was unusually fine. The ornament consisted predominantly of foliate motifs – carnations, tulips, narcissi, irises, hyacinths and dogroses. The fabrics were usually in delicate shades: pale blue, pale pink, light blue or light green with a gentle sheen of metallic thread.

In the centre of the showcase are two sticharions (a long vestment with wide sleeves) made of Persian fabric. One is of pale blue silk with carnations on long stems, the other, which belonged to Patriarch Adrian, is made of striped silk decorated with small irises and carnations.

Silk cloth woven with a very fine gold or silver thread was called altabas. The fabric was tight-woven and stiff, so garments made of altabas gave the impression of being cast from metal. The

226

□ **226. Saccos.** *Russia, 1322. Gold satin – Byzantium, late 13th century; Decorative embroidery – Russia, 14th century; Metal plates – Russia, 15th–17th century. Satin, gold and silver thread, pearls; embossing, embroidery, chasing, gilding. Belonged to Metropolitan Peter*

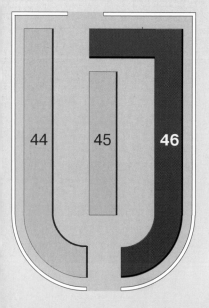

227

□ **227.** *"Small" saccos.* Byzantium, late 14th–
early 15th century. Gold satin, silver thread, silver,
pearls; embroidery.
Belonged to Metropolitan Photius

saccos of Patriarch Joachim (1674–1690) is made of Persian altabas.

There was also a great demand for Turkish fabrics in Russia in the 17th century. They are represented particularly fully in the Armoury collection. Turkish satins, velvets and altabases stand out for their decorativeness and bright colours. As in Persian fabrics, foliate ornament predominates, but the pattern is larger and more colourful. One often finds ornament in the form of twelve-pointed stars and carnations in full bloom. The pomegranate was regarded as a symbol of good fortune. The larger the pattern, the more highly the fabric was prized.

The deep red phelonion (a sleeveless vestment long at the front and short at the back) with a large gold moire pattern (seventh from the left) is made of Turkish satin. It was presented by Boris Godunov to the Archangel Cathedral in memory of Tsar Theodore, son of Ivan the Terrible, in 1602. The Kolomenskoye saccos of Patriarch Nikon, so called because it was presented to him by Tsar Alexis in 1653 in the village of

Kolomenskoye, is also made of Turkish satin.

The saccos of Patriarch Josaphat I is made of altabas. The white appliqué panels on the dark red background are woven with bouquets of carnations.

228

☐ **228. "Large" saccos.** *Russia, 1414–1417. Satin – Byzantium, early 14th century. Pictorial embroidery – Byzantium, 1414–1417. Decorative embroidery – Russia, 16th century. Satin, wire, gold and silver thread, pearls; embroidery. Belonged to Metropolitan Photius*

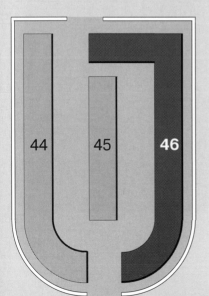

29

□ **229. *Saccos.*** *Moscow Kremlin Workshops,*
1654. Double looped axamite – Italy, 17th century.
Embroidery – Russia, late 16th – mid-17th century.
Axamite, gold, silver, gems, pearls; embroidery,
niello.
Belonged to Patriarch Nikon

Showcase 46
(Continued)

PRECIOUS FABRICS FROM ITALY, SPAIN, FRANCE AND RUSSIA

In the 16th and 17th centuries Russia's diplomatic relations with Western Europe expanded. The ambassadorial gifts which European diplomats brought for the Russian monarchs frequently included precious fabrics. Genoa, Florence and Venice were famed for their velvets, which had long been popular with Russian setters of fashion. Italian velvet was very tightly woven with a long pile and bright colours. The saccos of Metropolitan Macarius (1543–1564) made of mauve velvet with vertical gold stripes was presented by Ivan the Terrible to the Archangel Cathedral of the Moscow Kremlin in 1549.

The technique for weaving axamite velvets was a complex one. In the showcase you can see two saccoses

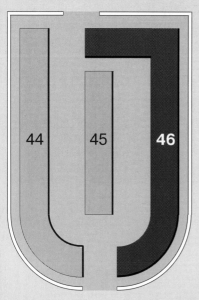

which belonged to Patriarch Adrian (1690–1700).

One was made in 1691 of a goldish-green Italian axamite velvet, the other in 1696 of red velvet with panels showing a coat-of-arms and a double-headed eagle under a crown. Fabrics of this kind were made in Italy and specially commissioned by the Russian court.

In the 17th century Venice specialised in making axamites, silk fabric closely interwoven with gold or silver. (The fine silk thread was actually twisted with a gold or silver thread). From the technical point of view it was very hard to make axamite. There were two types: smooth axamite, in which the background and ornament were woven on the same surface, and looped axamite. A specimen of a smooth axamite is the phelonion made in the Kremlin workshops with patterns of large flowers, rosettes and crowns, a present from Tsar Michael Romanov to Novospassky Monastery. The looped axamites were particularly hard to make. The pattern on them consisted of various types of gold loops, which formed a relief ornament and created a play of light and shade. The saccos of Patriarch Nikon (in the centre of the showcase) was made in 1654 of double-looped axamite. The saccos is adorned with 16th-century gold niello plates, large pearls and precious stones. It impressed people of the day greatly. The son of Patriarch Macarius of Antioch, the Syrian traveller Paul of Aleppo, who accompanied his father on a journey to Russia in 1655, wrote "Nikon took off his saccos, which was

230

□ **230. Saccos.** *Moscow, 1655. Linen, gold thread, pearls; embroidery. Belonged to Patriarch Nikon*

very hard to wear because of its weight. He had it made recently from pure gold brocade of a yellowish-walnut shade... Nikon invited us to pick it up, but we could not do so. They say there are some 36 lbs of pearls in it." The saccos does in fact weigh twenty-four kilograms. There are sixteen kilos of precious stones, etc. on it. It was worn on particularly solemn occasions even in the 18th century, for example, at the consecration of the SS Peter and Paul Cathedral in St Petersburg in 1752.

The showcase contains another, equally interesting saccos belonging to Patriarch Nikon, made in 1655. It looks as if it is made of expensive gold cloth, but this is not so. The saccos is actually made of ordinary linen. The illusion is created by the magnificent gold pattern embroidered by the skilful hands of Russian needlewomen. Patriarch Nikon's saccoses show that at the end of the 17th century the Russian Church rivalled even the tsar's court in luxury and wealth. Nikon died leaving about a hundred ceremonial vestments.

The saccos of Patriarch Philaret is made of Spanish axamite velvet. It was brought from Istanbul in 1623.

In the middle of the 17th century Italian fabrics began to be ousted by lighter French ones. About this time the fashion for lace trimming on female and male dress appeared, which explains why the ornament on French fabrics often reminds one of a lace pattern. Note the late 17th-century saccos in the showcase. The satin is interwoven with lacy garlands and bouquets of flowers. The light green background combines well with the white and pink pattern.

French fabrics had a complex colour range and rich patterns. At the end of the 17th century patterns of summer-houses, fountains and trees in little tubs appeared alongside foliate ornament of fruit, leaves and flowers.

Imported fabrics were very expensive, and the Moscow government frequently tried to set up the manufacture of precious fabrics in Russia. Regular production of fabrics in Russia did not begin until the 18th century, however, but it subsequently developed at such a rate that by the 19th century Russian brocades, silks and velvets were greatly prized by European monarchs and competed successfully with French fabrics on the European market and at international exhibitions.

The collection ends with a group of liturgical vestments made from Russian fabrics: velvet, silk and brocade of the 18th to early 19th centuries. As you have probably noticed, the ornament on Russian fabrics was quite varied. There was a fashion for striped and check material, garlands of lace and ribbons and patterns of roses. The ornament was sometimes entirely embroidered in pearls, which subdued the bright colours and made the garments look very special. This type of embroidery was popular in Russia, where it was known as far back as the 10th cen-

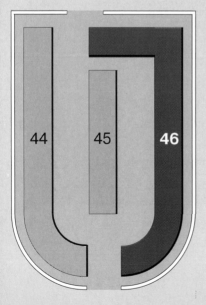

ury. The outline of the ornament, the inscriptions and the text of prayers were embroidered with pearls. The use of large and small pearls created the impression of relief ornament. The art of pearl embroidery was a difficult one, both technically and artistically. Surviving specimens testify to the remarkable skill of Russian embroideresses.

The phelonion (on the left) presented by Empress Catherine the Great to Metropolitan Platon is made of 18th-century Russian velvet. The velvet has unfortunately lost its original colour, red, but the pearl embroidery is very striking. The pearls were selected according to size and sewn onto a special thread, creating the impression of a raised relief ornament. The diamond-shaped pattern made up of elegant pearl sprays is executed in Russian classical style. The court gold-embroideress Darya Likhnovskaya worked on this phelonion for two years, adorning it with no less than 150,000 pearls. Catherine the Great's monogram embroidered on the phelonion was a rather bold violation of ecclesiastical canons, which required the depiction of the cross on church vestments; secular themes had begun to appear in the making of religious vestments.

231

☐ **231. Saccos.** *Moscow Kremlin Workshops, 1691. Velvet – Italy, 17th century. Velvet, silver, pearls, embroidery, casting, chasing. Belonged to Patriarch Adrian*

Showcase 46
(Continued)

PICTORIAL ARTISTIC EMBROIDERY

The specimens of artistic embroidery in this room cannot fail to attract attention. With the official adoption of Christianity in 988, together with the art of fresco- and icon-painting Russia received the art of pictorial embroidery, the aim of which was to depict saints and subjects from the Old and New testaments.

These specimens of embroidery are interesting because they frequently bear an inscription containing the name of the person who commissioned the article and sometimes of the embroidresses too, as well as the date and place where it was made, thereby providing valuable historical information.

Foreigners who visited Russia remarked that "The women here excel at exquisite embroidery in silk and gold."

If the article was a large one several embroidresses executed the work. The designs for the embroidery were done by special artists. The beauty of the embroidery depended not only on the design, however, but also on the needlewomen's skill in executing it, selecting fabric of the right colour for the background, combining silk threads with pearls, precious stones and gold and choosing the right stitches. Russian embroidresses knew up to a hundred different artistic stitches, which enabled them to create works of art that could rival icons and frescoes. Embroideresses could be found in every wealthy household: the homes of boyars, princes and merchants and also in convents.

The Kremlin Museums possess about two hundred works of pictorial embroidery. They include liturgical objects, such as altar cloths, veils, aers and shrouds. The content of the embroidery was determined by the object's function. Shrouds and aers were embroidered with the Entombment or Mourning of Christ, covers for church vessels with Our Lady of the Sign and veils with Russian saints.

The 14th-century church banner depicting an archangel with outspread wings on either side is one of the oldest surviving specimens of Russian embroidery. It is embroidered with spun gold thread. This is one type of pictorial embroidery. In the 15th century, however, embroidery in different coloured silks became particularly developed in Russia. One of the earliest

232

☐ **232. Cloth with the Virgin Mary Appearing
to the Venerable Sergius.** *Moscow, 15th century.
Damask – Italy, 15th century. 50.5×48*

ecimens in the Armoury collection is
e Puchezh shroud of 1441 depicting
e Entombment (top right). It got its
me from the town of Puchezh in
anovo Region, where it was found in
30. The shroud bears an embroi-
red inscription showing that it was
ecuted in Novgorod and connected
th the name of Archbishop Euthym-
s, known for his building activities in
that city. The colours of the silks have
been selected with great skill, from
dark tones to light ones, giving the figures an element of depth. The shroud
is also valuable because it can be dated
exactly and bears the name of the person who commissioned it.

The small veil embroidered with The
Blessed Virgin Appearing to the Venerable Sergius is typical of the end of

the century. Embroidered in coloured
silks, it depicts one of the most beloved
Russian compositions of the 16th century (top left).

In the 16th century there was increasing use of gold and silver thread in silk
embroidery. Among the leading workshops in the middle of the century
were those of the Staritsky princes.
The showcase contains a shroud depicting the Entombment, which was
presented by Princess Ephrosinia and
her son Vladimir to the Joseph-Vo-
lokolamsk Monastery in 1558. The
shroud is a fine specimen of the skill
and artistic taste of Russian needlewomen. Here they have created a true
work of art which conveys the pro-
found drama and expression inherent
in this mediaeval subject. In expres-
siveness such items rank with the finest
icons of their day.

The special skill of mediaeval portrai-
ture of real live people is demonstrated
by the palls depicting full-length
saints. There is an echo of Dionysius'
icons in the pall of light blue satin
dedicated to Metropolitan Peter (exe-

233

234

□ **234. Mitre.** *Moscow Kremlin Workshops, 163*
Gold, silver, gems, pearls; enamel, niello, embroi
dery, chasing. Height 22, diameter 20

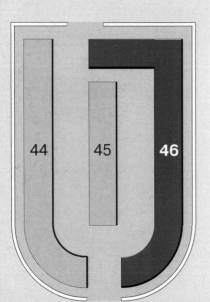

44 45 46

☐ **233. Mitre.**
*Moscow Kremlin
Workshops, 1682.
Gold, silver,
gems, pearls;
carving, gilding,
embroidery.
Height 26, diameter 21*
☐ **235. Phelonion.** *Moscow
Kremlin Workshops. Smooth
axamite – Italy,
17th century.
Decorative embroidery – Tsarina's workshop.
Axamite, gold,
silver, spun gold
thread, gems,
pearls; casting,
chasing, embroidery.
Donated by Tsar
Michael Romanov
to Novospassky
monastery*

235

ted in the workshop of Grand Prin-
ss Solomonia, the wife of Vassily III,
1512) and the pall "Metropolitan
exis" embroidered in 1581 in Tver.
e pall "St Zosima of Solovki" is an
ample of Russian mediaeval art cre-
ing an image which embodied the
eals of the day, the best things in
an, namely, serenity, inner concen-
ation, modesty and dignity.
ow the embroidresses managed to
nvey the complex compositions of
e iconography of their age is well il-
strated by the 1593 icon veil of the
d Testament Trinity with marginal
enes. Suffice it to say that the central

panel is based on Rublev's "Trinity",
which in itself speaks of good taste.
However, the urge to express their view
of the world led the creators of the veil
to an original treatment of the details.
Of particular interest in this respect are
the sixteen scenes embroidered round
the edges. In recreating the Old Testament view of the first days of the uni-
verse and treating the problem of God
and man, the veil, in the opinion of the
specialist N.A.Mayasova, conveys
"certain aspects of the philosophical
perception of God in 16th-century
Russia... On the one hand, He is the
giver of life, on the other, a chastising

force which casts down Satan from the heavens, expels sinners from Paradise and brings about the Flood and destruction of cities." The veil is typical of the 16th century with its philosophical strivings.

With the development of a national Russian market and the merchant class one finds an increasing number of items from the workshops of merchants and industrialists. The Stroganov workshops were particularly famous. Here you can see a 1657 pall of Metropolitan Jonah and a 1678 shroud which belonged to a rich Moscow merchant Ivan Guriev and repeats the composition on one of the Staritsky shrouds.

Ornamental embroidery was widespread in Russia as far back as pre-Christian times. Almost all the ceremonial robes and church vestments on display in this showcase are adorned with magnificent embroidery of pearls, precious stones and gold and silver plates. Nearly all these items were produced in the Kremlin chambers of the grand princes and tsars. The museums' collection contains about 500 pieces of ornamental embroidery.

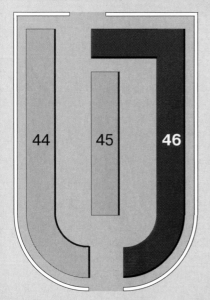

The style of embroidery changed over the centuries. It ceased to imitate painting. The main pattern depicted curving stems of plants with scrolls and shoots. In the 17th century more sumptuous embroidery appeared depicting flowers: carnations, tulips, pomegranate blossom, etc.

Pearls were a favourite ornament for Russian dress. Seed pearls were obtained in northern rivers and Lake Ilmen, while big pearls were brought from Caffa (now Feodosia). But the most prized were Hormuz pearls from the Hormuz strait (Persian Gulf).

Russian needlewomen were famed for their skill in threading pearls. At the end of the 16th century the Swedish traveller Petrei wrote of Russian women: "They are so experienced and skilled in embroidery that they excel many other pearl embroideresses and their works have been taken to distant lands."

Note the shoulder-piece of the phelonion and pallium of Patriarch Adrian. The richness of the fabric is enhanced by the embroidery in pearls and precious stones.

The black velvet shoulder-piece of the phelonion presented by Tsar Michael Romanov to Novospassky Monastery is embroidered with a rich pattern of pearls. The dense pearl sprays with small flowers of diamonds, rubies and emeralds on the shoulder-piece, the combination of large and small pearls on the hem, and the raised clear pattern remind one of chased metal. It was made in the Tsarina's chamber and is one of the finest specimens of 17th-century decorative embroidery.

The phelonion presented by Tsar Boris Godunov to the Archangel Cathedral of the Moscow Kremlin has gold plates with niello figures of saints and a pearl ornament of scrolls.

Embroidery often imitated the patterns on Turkish fabrics (e.g., the phelonion

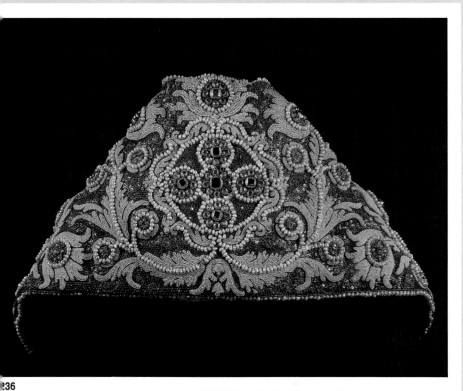

236

□ **236. Phelonion shoulder piece.** *Moscow Kremlin Workshops, 17th century. Velvet, gold, gems, pearls; casting, chasing, embroidery. Height 36, length 76*

of Patriarch Josaphat). The 1655 linen saccos of Patriarch Nikon, already mentioned above, a splendid example of gold embroidery, gives the impression of being made of gold cloth.

In the 18th century pearl embroidery was not so common, but individual pieces are remarkable for the number of pearls used and the beauty of the pattern. Thus, the phelonion of Metropolitan Platon made of Italian velvet is decorated with 150,000 pearls in the form of intertwining branches with Catherine the Great's monogram in the middle.

ROOM 7 ANCIENT STATE REGALIA

The state regalia, which at one time were an essential part of the ceremonial of royal processions and coronations, official and important ambassadorial receptions, have witnessed many historic events in bygone ages. The symbols of power has a special significance during the coronation ceremony.

Most of the exhibits date back to the 16th and 17th centuries, the time when the unification of the Russian lands around Moscow was being completed. Many items relating to official court life, such as the "cap of Monomachos", are world-famous.

The crowns, orbs, sceptres and thrones of Russian and foreign workmanship in our collection are true works of art and of great material value. From the accounts of foreign visitors the magnificence of the Moscow court made a great impression. Describing a reception given by Ivan the Terrible in January 1576, Chancellor Hans Cobenzel, the ambassador of the Holy Roman Emperor Maximilian II, remarked that the tsar and his son were dressed in robes studded with precious stones and had "rubies the size of a hen's egg burning like fire" on their headwear. "In all my life I have beheld such precious and splendid things... I have seen the crown and all the robes of the Catholic king, and of the Grand Duke of Tuscany, and I have seen many decorations of the King of France and His Imperial Majesty both in the kingdom of Hungary, and in Bohemia and other places. But, believe me, all that can in no way compare with what I saw here."

The tour begins with the thrones.

Showcases 47, 48, 49, 51   THRONES AND THRONE CHAIRS

237

□ **237. Throne.** *Persia, before 1604. Gold, gems, fabric, wood; flat chasing, embossing. Height 90, width 62.5, length 51.5. Present from Shah Abbas I of Persia to Tsar Boris Godunov in 1604*

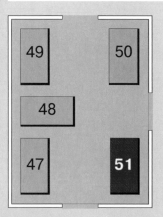

The earliest throne is a mid-16th century specimen of Renaissance culture. Pure white and very stable, it is made of wood faced with plates of ivory and walrus tusk. The carved ornament unites the various subjects and representations into a single composition. Among the scenes of historical, heraldic and everyday content the plates illustrating the life of King David who was greatly revered in Old Russia stand out in particular.

The throne is thought to have been made for the young Tsar Ivan IV, who

238

☐ **238. Throne.** *Western Europe, 16th century.*
Ivory, wood, fabric, metal; carving, casting, gilding.
Height 138, width 64, length 64.
Belonged to Tsar Ivan the Terrible

was crowned in 1547 at the age of seventeen.

Here too you can see a throne of oriental workmanship made at the end of the 16th century. It was presented by Shah Abbas I to Tsar Boris Godunov in 1604. The throne has a typically oriental form with a low back and arms. The master made use of ornament beloved in the East, namely, gold embossing, blue turquoises and red rubies. The back of the seat, the arms and the whole lower section of the throne were covered with gold Persian velvet. In 1742, when the throne was being prepared for the coronation, the old velvet was replaced by French velvet.

The throne of Tsar Michael, the first tsar of the Romanov dynasty, was made at the beginning of the 17th century from an old throne of oriental workmanship which had belonged to Ivan the Terrible. The Russian masters who remade it gave it the form of an old Russian armchair, with a high back and arms, but oriental motifs remain in the ornament. The throne is faced with embossed gold (no less than thirteen kilograms of the precious metal) and is adorned with turquoises, rubies, chrysolites, topazes and pearls.

One of the richest and most finely decorated thrones in our collection is the so-called Diamond throne presented to Tsar Alexis by an Armenian trading

239

□ **239. Throne.** Orient; Moscow Kremlin Workshops, before 1642. Gold, gems, pearls, fabric, wood; embossing, flat chasing. Height 154, width 75, length 52.
Belonged to Tsar Michael Romanov

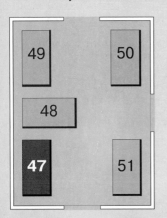

company in Persia for permission to trade without paying customs dues on the territory of Russia. In return for this throne the tsar gave the trading company 4,000 roubles in silver and 19,000 roubles in copper.

The throne is made of sandalwood faced with gold and silver plates on which there is a whimsical chased ornament of flowers and plants. Along the bottom is a band of carving with a bold pattern depicting a procession of elephants with drivers on their backs. On the back of the throne under the crown in a cartouche with a pearl frame is the following embroidered inscription: "For the most powerful and most invincible Emperor Alexis of Muscovy who doth reign felicitously upon the earth, this throne was made with great art, and may it be a token of future eternal bliss in heaven. In the year of Our Lord 1659".

An intricate mosaic of turquoises and diamonds (about 900 in all) covers the whole surface of the throne, making it quite priceless.

A unique situation arose in Russia at the end of the 17th century, when two tsareviches were crowned together. Tsar Alexis died leaving three sons. The eldest, Theodore, ruled very briefly and died unexpectedly in 1682. According to the law of succession the next eldest son, fifteen-year-old Ivan, should have inherited the throne, but he was feeble-minded and in poor health. So it was decided to crown the two brothers together, Ivan and ten-year-old Peter (the future Peter the Great). And a double-seated throne was made specially for the occasion. None too sure of the young monarchs' ability to decide matters of state, the boyars had a secret hiding-place built in the back of the throne for the boys' mentors. More often than not this was occupied by their elder sister Sophia, who was twenty-five and quite educated for her day: she knew Latin and

240

☐ **240. Diamond throne.** *Persia, 1659. Gold, silver, gems, pearls, fabric, wood; casting, chasing, carving, embossing, pictorial and decorative embroidery, lacquered miniatures on wood. Height 161, width 75.5, length 51.*
Presented to Tsar Alexis by an Armenian trading company

□ **241. Double throne.** *Moscow Kremlin Work-shops, 1682–1684. Silver, wood; casting, chasing, carving, engraving, gilding. Height about 400, width 215, length 182, depth of seat 84.*
Belonged to tsars Ivan and Peter, sons of Alexis

241

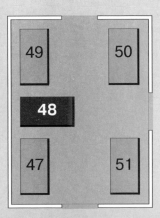

49	50
48	
47	51

Greek and could play several musical instruments.

During receptions of foreign envoys Sophia would whisper answers to envoys' questions from the hiding-place through a little window covered with a cloth to Peter, who was a clever boy. The foreigners were often amazed at the quick-wittedness of the ten-year-old tsar.

Noteworthy in the varied ornament on the throne are the silver and gold plates with chased figures of fantastic gryphons, unicorns, snow leopards and lions. In mediaeval symbolism these are the signs of power and authority. These symbols are found in Russian art as far back as the 12th century, beginning with the decor of the famous Vladimir cathedrals. The turning to national images takes place in the new dynamic and restless style of Russian baroque.

In addition to the collection of 16th- and 17th-century thrones, there are also some throne chairs. They were used at coronations and other special occasions. The most interesting are the 18th-century throne chairs of Empress Elizabeth (1742) and Emperor Paul I (1796).

A specimen of the art of the following stage (the transition from baroque to rococo) is the throne chair of Empress Elizabeth, daughter of Peter the Great. While preserving a solemn majesty, it is also very elegant and attractive. The curved legs and arms are adorned not only with carved flowers and grasses, but also with charming female heads. The throne's official function is emphasised by the splendid decorative embroidery on the back with the state emblem and Elizabeth's monogram. This combination of the insignia of power with the whimsical elegance of the carved wooden scrolls is indicative of the fact that the throne belonged to a woman.

242

□ **242. Throne.** *St Petersburg, 1740–1742. Wood, fabric; carving, gilding, decorative embroidery. Height 212, width 100, length 76. Belonged to Empress Elizabeth, daughter of Peter the Great*

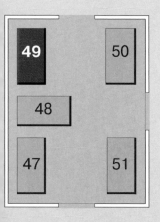

Showcase 50	ANCIENT STATE REGALIA AND CEREMONIAL ITEMS

The showcase contains insignia of monarchical power and tsarist regalia, which are fine specimens of jewellery of the 13th to 18th centuries and of great value for the history of the Russian state.

On the right you can see the famous cap of Monomachus, which was used to crown all the Russian tsars up to Peter the Great. The cap is of oriental workmanship of the late 13th and early 14th century. It is still not known for sure where and by whom this masterpiece of jewellery was made. The oldest section of the crown consists of eight gold plates adorned with very fine gold lace in a pattern of six-pointed rosette-stars and lotus blossoms. The semi-spherical top with a cross, the sable trimming and the pearls and precious stones belong to a later period. The crown weighs 698 grammes and is the lightest of all those in the showcase.

There are several legends about the cap of Monomachus. The mediaeval *Tale of the Princes of Vladimir* says that Emperor Constantine Monomachus of Byzantium presented his grandson, Prince Vladimir of Kiev, with the crown from his head. This crown is said to have been worn and handed down by the princes first of Kiev, then of Vladimir and finally of Moscow. Thus, the cap of Monomachus symbolised the continuity of power of the Moscow tsars from the emperors of Byzantium.

The well-known Soviet historian K.V.Bazilevich has established that the cap of Monomachus is first mentioned in the 14th-century will of Grand Prince Ivan Kalita of Moscow, but was simply called a "gold cap". It only began to be called the cap of Monomachus two hundred years later in the will of Tsar Ivan the Terrible, when the idea of Moscow as the third Rome was popular. Bazilevich believes that the cap of Monomachus was presented to Ivan Kalita by Khan Uzbek of the Golden Horde. It was customary at that time for Russian princes to travel to the Golden Horde with rich presents, in return for which they received equally sumptuous gifts.

The first documentary references to a coronation at which the cap of Monomachus was used date back to 1498. The last time the cap was used for this purpose was in 1682, when two tsars, Ivan and Peter, were crowned at the same time. The eldest son Ivan was crowned with the cap of Monomachus of the "first set", while Moscow craftsmen made a "second-set" replica of the cap for Peter. It was similar in form to the old one, but inferior in artistic qualities. There was a rule that the cap of Monomachus should be worn only once in a lifetime, during the coronation. For other solemn occasions each tsar had his own ceremonial crown.

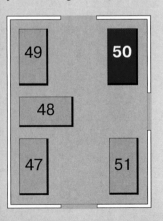

□ **243. Crown of Monomachus.** *Orient, late 13th – early 14th century. Gold, silver, gems, pearls, fur; filigree, seeds of gold, casting, chasing, engraving. Height 18.6, circumference 61*

243

The showcase contains several royal crowns. On the right of the cap of Monomachus is a crown which belonged to Ivan the Terrible and is known as the cap of the realm of Kazan. There are many legends about it. One says that the cap of Kazan could have belonged to the last khan of Kazan, Ediger Mahmet, who was baptised in Moscow in 1553 and received the title of ruler of Kazan. Specialists believe that Ivan probably commissioned Moscow craftsmen to make it after the capture of Kazan, but with the help of craftsmen from Kazan. The gold crown is made of open-work medallions, or *gorodki*, of different sizes and shapes, adorned with almandines, turquoises and pearls. The gold surface of the crown is covered with a dense niello pattern of foliate ornament.

☐ **244. Crown of Kazan.** *Russia, mid-16th century. Gold, gems, fur; casting, chasing, carving, niello. Height 24.8, circumference 65*

☐ **245. "Grand Set".** *Late 16th – first third of 17th century. Crown – Moscow Kremlin Workshops, 1627. Orb – Western Europe, late 16th century. Sceptre – Western Europe, c. 1600. Gold, gems, pearls, fur; casting, chasing, engraving, carving, enamel, flat chasing. Crown – height 30.2, circumference 66.5. Orb – height 42.4. Sceptre – 70.5, diameter 17 (minimum), 25 (maximum). Belonged to Tsar Michael Romanov*

244

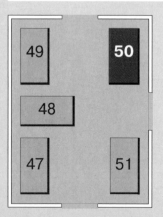

The cap of Monomachus and the cap of the realm of Kazan are the oldest crowns to have survived.

In 1627–1628 the finest jewellers in the Kremlin workshops together with foreign masters under the supervision of state secretary Efim Telepnyov made the objects in Michael Romanov's "Grand Set": a crown, orb, sceptre and bow-and-arrow case, which are first-class specimens of jewellery.

The gold crown is decorated with rows of open-work medallions, or *gorodki*, with emeralds, rubies and splendid sapphires.

245

The relief surface of the crown is covered with white, blue and green enamel. The orb, the symbol of Christianity triumphant, is crowned with a four-pointed cross. It bears high relief enamelled scenes from the life of King David (The Anointment of David by the Prophet Samuel, David's Victory Over Goliath, David Returning After the Victory and The Persecution By Saul). The emeralds, sapphires, rubies and pearls are all in high frames.

In the 1650s Tsar Alexis commissioned Istambul jewellers to make a new set of royal regalia consisting of an orb, a sceptre and a humeral. The gold surface of these items is lavishly adorned with flat precious stones, diamonds, rubies, sapphires and emeralds, as well as enamelled medallions.

The humeral is very fine with its large medallions. There are seven of them. The enamelled scenes from Christian history are framed by precious stones.

In 1682–1689 diamond crowns were made for the two brothers, Ivan and Peter. Hundreds of large and small diamonds arranged in the form of flowers,

246

□ **246.** *Dia-mond crown.* *Moscow Kremlin Workshops, 1682–1687. Gold, silver, gems, pearls, fur; casting, chasing, carving, enamel. Height 28.3, circumference 65. Belonged to Tsar Peter the Great*

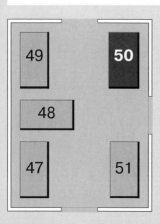

leaves, crowns and double-headed eagles create a glittering play of light.

Pectoral decorations, such as crosses, panagias and chains, were an essential part of ceremonial attire.

The showcase contains chains made with remarkable skill, such as the one consisting of eighty-eight flat rings decorated with niello, enamel and a carved inscription of Tsar Michael Romanov's full title.

The showcase also contains the state sword and shield. They began to be used as part of the royal regalia at the end of the 17th century.

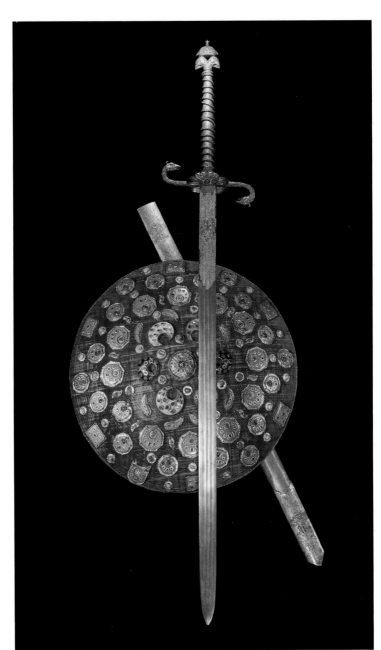

□ **247. State sword and shield.** *Sword – Moscow, late 17th century. Silver, steel, gold brocade, wood; casting, chasing, carving, engraving, gilding. Length 141. Shield – Moscow, late 17th century. Gold, silver, gems, fabric; casting, chasing, carving, embossing, embroidery. Diameter 58.4*

247

□ **248. Crown of Monomachus (second set).** *Moscow Kremlin Workshops, 1682. Gold, gems, pearls, fur; casting, chasing, carving. Height 20.3, circumference 61*

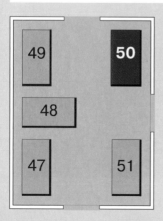

The shield is round and made of wood covered with red velvet and adorned with figured appliqué work of jade and rock crystal, inlaid precious stones and bright enamel.

Note the book entitled *On the Election of Tsar Michael Romanov to the Most High Throne of the Russian Realm*. It was commissioned by Tsar Alexis Romanov from craftsmen in the Armoury and Ambassadorial Office who did the work under the supervision of the head of the Ambassadorial Office, the boyar A.S. Matveyev. The manuscript text is written in black

249. Crown. St Petersburg, 1730–1731. Master; G.W.Dunkel. Silver, gold, gems; casting, chasing, carving, gilding. Height 1.3, circumference 68

249

Indian ink and the twenty-one miniatures illustrating official receptions, ceremonies and court life in the 17th century are executed in gold, silver and coloured paint.

Under Peter the Great Russia was declared an empire in 1721. The coronation rite was changed, the old type of cap-crown being replaced by an ordinary crown and the humeral by a special mantle called a *porphyra*. The first coronation of the new type took place in 1724. Peter himself placed the crown and imperial mantle on his wife Catherine I.

The showcase contains a crown which belonged to Empress Anne and is one of the first new-type Russian crowns. It is made of silver and adorned with about 2,500 diamonds and an enormous tourmaline. The form was to become traditional: two open-work hemispheres divided by a movable arc with a cross in the middle and a broad circlet. The crown was made by Gottlieb Wilhelm Dunkel in St Petersburg in 1731.

ROOM 8

CEREMONIAL HORSE HARNESS OF THE 16TH TO 18TH CENTURIES

The collection of the Stables Treasury occupies an important place among the Armoury collections.

The saddles, horse-cloths and chest bands (a chest strap fastened to the saddle at both ends) on display here all differ in technique of workmanship and ornament. In size and artistic qualities the collection is unique. Nearly all these items were made in the Kremlin workshops of the Royal Stables.

In the 16th and 17th centuries great political importance was attached to ceremonial horse harness, royal mounted processions and the meeting of foreign ambassadors. The richer the procession, the mightier the state would seem in the eyes of foreign envoys. The Stables Treasury came under the Royal Stables Office, which was set up at the end of the 15th century and was in charge of mounted processions, horses, harness and carriages. The Office was run by the senior equerry, a boyar who was the highest official in the state after the tsar. Boris Godunov once held this post.

How rich the Royal Stables Office was can be seen from the fact that in the 17th century it had charge of 150 saddle-, carriage and sledge horses for the tsar; 52 for the tsarina and tsarevnas; 100 for envoys; 3,000 fine horses for royal processions and over 40,000 for military campaigns.

The Royal Stables Office had special workshops in which silversmiths made bits, stirrups and silver jingling chains; jewellers adorned the items with precious stones and pearls; needlewomen made sledge rugs, horse-cloths, *chaldars* (horse-cloths that covered the

horse's croup, flanks and chest); and goldsmiths, enamellers, chasers and engravers decorated the saddles.

At the end of the 17th century a special building was erected for the Royal Stables Office in the Kremlin by Borovitsky Gate on the spot where the Ar-

moury now stands. It remained there until the middle of the 19th century. In the 18th century the Royal Stables Office was reorganised as the Stables Chancellery and Office, and the objects kept in the Royal Stables Treasury were handed over to the Armoury in 1736.

Showcase 52

RUSSIAN HORSE HARNESS OF THE 16TH TO 18TH CENTURIES

This showcase contains items made in the Royal Stables Office of the Kremlin in the 16th and 17th centuries. There was great demand abroad for saddles made by Russian craftsmen. The form of the Russian saddle did not restrict the rider's movements, but allowed him to use his weapons easily and fire without stopping his horse. Note the form of Ivan the Terrible's saddle. The broad pommel curves strongly inwards. The saddle is covered with cherry-coloured velvet embroidered with gold and silver double-headed eagles and unicorns amid a foliate ornament. The pommel and cantle are adorned with chased gold plates with precious stones.

The saddle of Boris Godunov is decorated with very finely engraved fantastic birds, grasses and flowers on the silver frame and lion masks on the curves. In 1637–1638 the master Ivan Popov and "companions" made a ceremonial saddle for Tsar Michael Romanov. The gold pommel and cantle are decorated with multicoloured enamel, emeralds, rubies, sapphires and diamonds. The seat is covered with Italian looped axamite (top left).

250

Special holsters were attached to saddles to hold pistols. The holsters in the showcase are bound with red velvet and decorated with pearl embroidery. The saddle and stirrups of Prince D.I.Pozharsky which he took on his military campaigns are simple in form and modest in ornament. The saddle is covered with cherry-coloured velvet fixed down by a silver pommel and cantle which emphasise its attractive silhouette. Here you can see a processional horse in a full set of ceremonial harness.

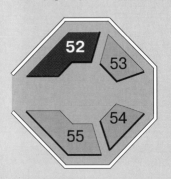

251

☐ **250. Saddle.** *Moscow Kremlin Workshops, 1637. Master: I.Popov "with companions". Gold, wood, velvet; carving, enamel, weaving. Height of pommel 30, height of cantle 21, length 49*

☐ **251. Full set of ceremonial horse harness.** *Moscow, 17th century. Plume, bridle, frontlet, jingling chain, neck tassel, saddle, chest band. Brocade, gems, gold, silver; filigree, chasing*

252

☐ **252. Saddle.** *Moscow Kremlin Workshops,*
1682. Masters: L.Mymrin, S.Fedotov, L.Afanasiev.
Silver, wood, velvet; enamel, filigree, weaving.
Height of pommel 23, height of cantle 17, length 46

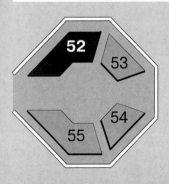

These horses were led before the tsar's
carriage. There were sometimes over a
hundred of them. The horses wore a
horse-cloth of velvet or brocade embroidered with precious stones and
pearls, a head-stall decorated with
enamel and precious stones, a neck tassel threaded with pearls and a special
saddle on which no one ever sat, because the cushion on it was embroidered with pearls and precious stones.

253. **Harness for parade horse.** Plume, bridle, frontlet, neck tassel, jingling chain, saddle, chest band, horse cloth, stirrups, knee-guards. Moscow, 17th century. Brocade, gems, gold, silver; filigree, chasing, carving, enamel, weaving

253

The horses were linked to one another by silver chains. When the whole procession was in motion, the glitter of the gold and gems and the jingle of the silver chains made an unforgettable impression.

Watching a royal procession in 1675 the Polish diplomat Swiderski said that in no other neighbouring state could you find horses so richly attired.

Meetings to receive foreign envoys and processions of pilgrimage were extremely sumptuous. For example, no less than 5,287 people took part in meeting the Persian envoy Assan-Bek in 1640, including 1,000 musketeers on "horses from the Royal Stables".

Showcases 53,54

TURKISH CEREMONIAL HARNESS OF THE 18TH CENTURY

In the late 18th century following the end of the first Russo-Turkish war, in which Turkey was defeated, Sultan Abdul Hamid sent Catherine the Great a saddle with a full set of ceremonial harness, sabres and a *pernat*. The war ended in 1774 and the gift was presented a year later, in 1775, on the occasion of the treaty of Kuchuk Kainarji under which Russia gained access to the Black Sea and the right for her trading vessels to sail through the Dardanelles.

254

□ **254. Plume-holder.** *France, 18th century. Gold, brilliants; enamel, chasing, carving. Height 16,5.*
From the present of the Turkish Sultan Abdul Hamid I to Empress Catherine the Great in 1775
□ **255. Ceremonial harness for tsar's horse.** *Head-stall, chest band, saddle, horse-cloth, front-let, pernat. Turkey, 18th century. Gold, silver, brilliants, coral, lazurite, brocade; chasing.*
From the resent of the Turkish Sultan Abdul Hamid I to Empress Catherine the Great in 1775

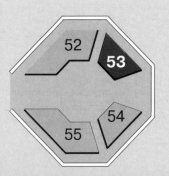

THE ARMOURY

All the items in this set are made of
gold and silver and incrusted with a
large number of precious stones. The
plume-holder alone is decorated with
1,030 diamonds, which are set off by a
magnificent goldenish Brazil topaz.
The gifts include a silver horse bucket
and silver horseshoes with silver nails.
The horse-cloth of silver brocade is
embroidered with coral and lazurite.
The second Russo-Turkish war ended
like the first with the victory of the
Russian army, under A.V.Suvorov and
F.F.Ushakov. And again the Turkish
sultan, this time Selim III, sent a rich
set of harness after the conclusion of
the Treaty of Jassy. All the items in it
were made of gold and adorned with
diamonds, rubies and emeralds. The
horse-cloth was embroidered with gold
thread and small plates with diamonds
and rubies.

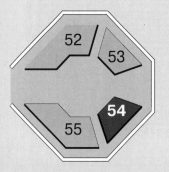

□ **256. Harness
for parade
horse.** *Head-
stall, chest band,
saddle, horse-
cloth, frontlet,
stirrups, mace,
sabre in scab-
bard. Turkey, late
18th century.
Gold, gems, bro-
cade; chasing,
weaving.
Present from the
Turkish Sultan Se
lim III to Empress
Catherine the
Great in 1793*

Showcase 55	PERSIAN, TURKISH AND EUROPEAN CEREMONIAL HARNESS OF THE 16TH AND 17TH CENTURIES

Some extremely rich horse harness came to Russia as gifts from Eastern countries, namely, Persia, Turkey, China and Bukhara, with which Russia had trading and diplomatic relations. The horse was greatly respected in the East. There is an Eastern saying that "My horse is my friend, nay, he is better than a friend" and "A falcon in the sky is helpless without wings, and a man on earth is powerless without a horse."

Here you can see items of ceremonial horse harness made in Persia in the 16th and 17th centuries which came to Russia as gifts from shahs, envoys and merchants. Already in the 15th century Persian merchants were carrying on a lively trade with Russia, but diplomatic relations with Persia were not established until the 16th century.

In 1590 Shah Abbas I of Persia sent Tsar Theodore of Russia a gold saddle covered with velvet and adorned with a large bright blue turquoise, rubies and emeralds.

Noteworthy among the exhibits in the showcase is the Persian velvet woven with carnations on the gold saddle of

Tsar Michael Romanov, a present from Shah Safi (1635). The saddle is studded with pearls, rubies, emeralds and turquoises, a very popular stone in the East.

Persian horse-cloths were made of silk, brocade and velvet and decorated with silver and gold embroidery. Some were made of linen, in which case they were embroidered all over with gold and silver to imitate brocade.

The group of Turkish exhibits is the largest in the showcase. Turkish saddles are broader at the base than Persian and Russian ones, fit more closely to the horse's back and have a high pointed pommel at the front and a sloping cantle at the back. Turkish masters made saddles of gilded silver embellished with niello, engraving and chasing. The velvet and altabas covering was embroidered with flowers composed of pearls and precious stones.

Here too you can see items of ceremonial horse harness made by Polish, English, Czech and German craftsmen. The earliest items in the collection are the Polish hussar saddles. They were presented to Boris Godunov in 1600 by the ambassador of King Sigismund III of Poland. The hussar saddles fit the horse's back closely, a typical feature of West-European saddles, while the high sloping head of the pommel was borrowed from the East.

The Polish *archak* (a small saddle with a detachable cushion) which belonged to Prince Stefan Mossalsky is a 17th-century specimen. It is covered with red velvet, and the pommel and cantle are silvered and gilded.

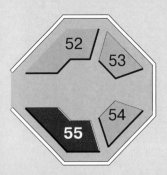

Ceremonial horse harness. Turkey, 17th century

The splendid saddle by the well-known master Andjei Makenzen I was presented to the Russian tsar by an embassy from Stanislaw Wenslawski in 1651. It is covered with gold-embroidered raspberry-coloured velvet. The silver pommel is topped by a lion's head. Note the chest band made by the Prague master Ioann Mikhael. The pearls, precious stones and blue enamel create an impression of elegance. It is thought to have been a present to Tsar Boris Godunov by the Holy Roman Emperor Rudolph II.

The German saddles in the showcase (second half of 17th century) have the traditional form which developed in the age of chivalry and are meant for a firm seat, which is why their pommels are steep, like armchairs. The saddles had special clips for the legs. The main ornament was splendid high-relief embroidery.

ROOM 9

CARRIAGES OF THE 16TH TO 18TH CENTURIES

The collection of carriages in the Armoury is one of the finest in the world. In many respects it is unique.

Our collection makes it possible to trace the development of carriage-making in Russia and Western Europe. Its value lies in the fact that all the carriages have survived more or less in their original form and the names of their owners and makers are known, such as John Buckendal, Johann Hoppenhaupt, Nicolas Pineau, François Boucher and Philippe Caffieri. The forms, constructions and decor changed over the 16th to 18th centuries.

Carriages had been known in Russia since early times. A 15th-century chronicle contains a reference to carriages used by princes. They were covered sledges upholstered on the inside with velvet, linen or fur. In the 16th and 17th centuries carriages were made in the workshops of the tsar's and patriarch's courts. The materials used were oak, walnut, beech, ash, maple and alder wood. The numerous carriages and sledges, open and closed were placed in the charge of the Royal Stables Office in the Moscow Kremlin. Up to the 19th century carriages were used by a very narrow circle of people.

The oldest carriage in the collection is a late 16th-century specimen from England, a present to Boris Godunov from King James I of England in 1603. The carriage is still simple in form. Its construction and technical system are still imperfect, and it has no turning wheel. A great deal of space was needed to turn the carriage round, and on sharp turns the wheels had to be moved by hand. There is no driver's seat. The

257

□ **257. Carriage.** *England, late 16th – early 17th century. Wood, oils, velvet; wood carving, gilding, painting, weaving. Height 250, width 230, length 540.*
Present from King James I of England to Tsar Boris Godunov in 1603

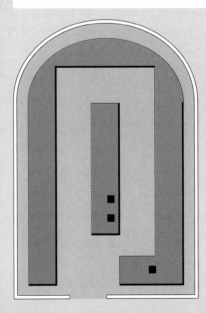

horses were led by the bridle or the driver mounted the leading horse.

This type of open carriage without springs or a turning wheel was called a *kolymaga* in Russia. The carriage's ornament is interesting — high-relief wood carving showing battles between Christians and Moslems and hunting scenes.

Next to it is a Russian-made closed carriage of the first half of the 17th century. It is upholstered in raspberry-coloured velvet and decorated with an ornament of copper nails. The carriage bears the coat-of-arms of its first owner, the mayor of the town of Bryansk, Nikita Ivanovich Romanov. This carriage is depicted on V.I.Surikov's famous canvas *The Morning of the Streltsys' Execution* now in the Tretyakov Gallery.

258

☐ **258. Winter "amusement" sledge.** *Moscow Kremlin Stables Workshops, 1689–1692. Wood, leather, taffeta, tin, copper, mica; embossing, gilding. Height 120, width 72, length 150. Belonged to Tsarevna Catherine, Peter the Great's niece*

☐ **259. Summer "amusement" carriage.** *Moscow Kremlin Stables Workshops, 1690–1692. Oak, leather, taffeta, tin, mica; stamping, gilding. Height 140, width 75, length 180. Belonged to Tsarevich Alexis, son of Peter the Great*

259

THE ARMOURY

□ **260. Garden carriage.** *Russia, second quarter of 17th century. Wood, velvet; oil painting, gilding on gesso, wood carving. Height 150, width 140, length 310.*
Belonged to Empress Anne

□ **261. Carriage.** *St Petersburg, 1739. Wood, velvet, gold thread, bronze; oil painting, gilding on gesso, wood carving, weaving, embroidery. Height 260, width 200, length 500.*
Belonged to Empress Anne

260

261

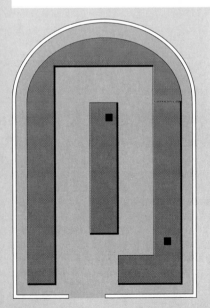

The 17th-century children's summer and winter sledges made by Kremlin craftsmen are upholstered in embossed leather and have mica windows. The summer sledge has a swivel pin and a "swan's neck". The summer sledge belonged to Peter the Great's son, Alexis, and the winter sledge to the daughter of Tsar Ivan (Peter's half-brother and co-ruler).

The two-seated carriage made for Empress Anne by St Petersburg craftsmen

in 1739 represented a step forward in carriage-making. It has springs concealed behind bronze ornaments, a turning wheel and a driver's box. There is pane glass in the windows.

The so-called Holstein carriage was made by French craftsmen at the beginning of the 18th century. Prince Friedrich of Holstein, the fiancé of Peter the Great's daughter Anne, is thought to have come to St Petersburg in it. The carriage has cranked springs, a swivel pin, a driver's box and footboards for footmen.

In mediaeval Russia sledges were used from very early times, in summer as well as winter. Only boyars and members of the higher clergy had the right to travel by sledge in summer and not in a carriage on wheels.

In this room you can see the open garden carriage of Empress Anne made by craftsmen in the Royal Stables Office. The carriage has low wheels with broad rims so as not to spoil the garden paths.

Note the 18th-century winter sledge by Moscow craftsmen. It is in the form of a wagon on runners. The inside is upholstered in green cloth and there are benches along the sides. In the middle is a long table with two silver braziers. It was in this sledge that Peter the Great's daughter, Elizabeth, travelled from St Petersburg to Moscow for her coronation in 1742.

The sledge was drawn by twenty-three horses harnessed in seven groups of three with two horses leading. Elizabeth changed literally hundreds of horses on the way, so anxious was she to accede to the Russian throne.

Nearby are two carriages which also belonged to Elizabeth and were made by Viennese craftsmen in 1740–1742. They are closed, two-seater ones of the coupé type. The body was suspended on two leather thongs and swayed a lot when in motion. One of the carriages is decorated with rococo-style woodcarving, the other with painting. The carving is covered with a thick layer of gilt and bright paint.

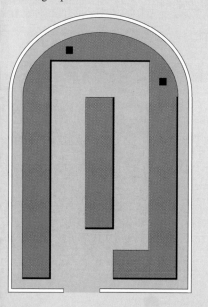

□ **262. Carriage.** *Austria, Vienna, 1741–1742. Wood, velvet, bronze; wood carving, gilding on gesso, painting, weaving, casting, chasing. Height 280, width 260, length 550. Belonged to Empress Elizabeth, daughter of Peter the Great*

□ **263. Carriage.** *Austria, Vienna, 1740. Wood, velvet, bronze; wood carving, gilding on gesso, oil painting, weaving, casting, chasing. Height 270, width 250, length 550. Belonged to Empress Elizabeth, daughter of Peter the Great*

262

263

264

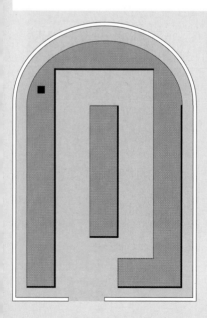

Note the splendid carriage made by the Berlin craftsman Johann Michael Hoppenhaupt in 1746. It gives an impression of lightness and elegance thanks to the skilful woodcarving depicting laurel leaves, scrolls, shells and sculptures of mythological deities. Rococo features are clearly evident in the form of the body and in the decor. The body is suspended on six leather thongs and has springs and a turning wheel. The carriage was a gift to Empress Elizabeth from Friedrich II. It was used during coronation festivities, which explains why it was renovated so many times.

265

□ **264–265. Carriage and detail.** *Germany, Berlin, 1746. Master: J.M.Hoppenhaupt. Wood, velvet, paste; wood carving, gilding on gesso, weaving. Height 200, width 250, length 550.*

Present from King Frederick II of Prussia to Empress Elizabeth, daughter of Peter the Great

266

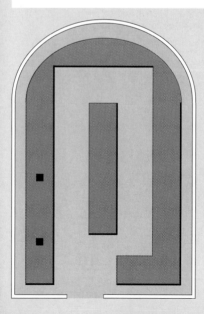

The four-seater carriage made by the French master A.Drillerosse from a design by the architect Nicolas Pineau is very luxurious. The exquisite bronze ornaments were made in the workshop of Philippe Caffieri. The painting on it is by the well-known 18th-century French court painter François Boucher. The carriage was a gift to Empress Elizabeth from Kirill Razumovsky, the hetman of the Ukraine. It has survived without any restoration.

In the second half of the 18th century carriages became technically more advanced. The bodies were suspended on four leather thongs making them more stable in motion. Vertical metal springs made it possible to raise the body higher off the ground, which was most important given the state of roads at that

267

□ **266. Carriage.** *France, Paris, 1763–1765. Ashwood, velvet, mother-of-pearl, bronze; oil painting, gilding on gesso, wood carving. Height 250, width 225, length 450.*
Belonged to Empress Catherine the Great
□ **267. Berlin carriage.** *St Petersburg, 1769. Master: J.C.Buckendal. Wood, velvet, bronze, paste; painting, gilding on gesso, wood carving, chasing, casting. Height 240, width 250, length 560.*
Belonged to Empress Catherine the Great

time. The travelling carriage of Catherine the Great made in Paris in 1763 by the Berlin craftsman Breiteil is of this type. The body is adorned with painting on mythological subjects. Catherine travelled to the Crimea in this carriage.

The most technically advanced equipage in the collection is the four-seated ceremonial carriage made in St Petersburg by John Coenrad Buckendal for Catherine the Great. It has both vertical and horizontal springs.

268

□ **268. Summer carriage.** *England, 1770s.*
Wood, oil, velvet; wood carving, gilding on gesso,
painting, weaving. Height 240, width 190, length
410.
Present from Count G. Orlov to Empress Catherine
the Great

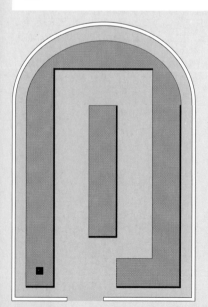

The summer carriage in the form of an
Italian gondola was made in England
in the 1770s. It was a present to Empress Catherine the Great from Count
Orlov. The carriage is adorned with
magnificent woodcarving of laurel and
oak leaves, flower garlands, banner
and trophies and covered with a thin
layer of gold. It gives the impression of
being carved metal. This carriage is artistically one of the finest in the world.

INDEX OF RUSSIAN NAMES MENTIONED IN THE TEXT

Adrian *(1636–1700), the last Russian patriarch (1690). Peter the Great abolished the patriarchate after his death*
Alexander I *(1777–1825), Russian Emperor (1801), the eldest son of Paul I*
Alexander II *(1818–1881) – Russian Emperor (1855), the eldest son of the Emperor Nicholas I.*
Alexander III *(1845–1894), Russian Emperor (1881), the second son of Alexander II*
Alexander Nevsky *(c. 1220–1263), Grand Prince of Vladimir (1252), statesman and military leader. Canonised in 13th century*
Alexandra Fyodorovna *(1798–1860), Russian Empress, the wife of Nicholas I and daughter of King Frederick William III of Prussia*
Alexandra Fyodorovna *(1872–1918), Russian Empress, the wife of Nicholas II and daughter of the Grand Duke of Hessen.*
Alexis *(1290s–1378), Metropolitan of Kiev and All Russia. Canonised in the 15th century*
Alexis *(1629–1676), the second Russian tsar (1645) of the Romanov dynasty*
Alexis *(1654–1670), the eldest son of Tsar Alexis*
Alexis *(1690–1718), the son of Peter the Great. Renounced his right to the throne*
Anne *(1693–1740), the daughter of Tsar Ivan V, son of Alexis. Duchess of Courland (1711) and Russian Empress (1730)*

Anne *(1708–1728), the daughter of Peter the Great and Catherine I. Mother of Emperor Peter III*

Bagration Peter Ivanovich *(1765–1812), prince, hero of the Patriotic War against Napoleon*
Basil I *(1371–1425), Grand Prince of Moscow and Vladimir (1389), the son of Dmitri Donskoy*
Basil II (the Blind) *(1415–1462), Grand Prince of Moscow (1425), the father of Ivan III*
Basil III *(1479–1533), Grand Prince of Moscow (1505), the son of Ivan III*
Boris Godunov *(c. 1552–1605), virtual ruler of Russia (1584–1598), Russian tsar (1598)*

Catherine I *(Marta Skavronskaya) (1684–1727), daughter of a Lithuanian peasant, wife of Peter the Great (1712) and Empress of Russia (1725)*
Catherine II (the Great) *(1729–1796), born Princess Sophia of Anhalt-Zerbst, wife of the heir apparent, the future Peter III (1745) and Empress of Russia (1762)*
Cyril of Belozersk *(1337–1427), Russian churchman and politician, writer, archimandrite of the Simonov monastery in Moscow (1388–1390), founder of the St Cyril of Belozersk monastery (1397), canonised in the 16th century*

Dionysius *(?–1385), Archbishop of Suzdal, he had ambitions to become Metropolitan of Moscow*

Dmitri *(1708–1767), Archbishop of Novgorod who officiated at Catherine the Great's coronation (1762), after which he was appointed metropolitan*
Dmitri Ivanovich Donskoy *(1350–1389), grand prince of Moscow and Vladimir (1362), military leader*
Dmitri Ivanovich *(1581–1591), tsarevich, son of Ivan the Terrible and his seventh wife, Maria Nagaya. Died in Uglich. Canonised in the 17th century*
Dmitri-Foma Konstantinovich *(1323–1384), grand prince of Nizhny Novgorod, ally of the princes of Moscow*

Elizabeth *(1709–1762), the daughter of Peter the Great and Catherine, Empress of Russia (1741)*
Euthymius II *(?–1458), Archbishop of Novgorod (1429)*

Godunov Dmitri Ivanovich *(?–1605), boyar at the court of Ivan the Terrible, the uncle of Boris Godunov.*
Golitsyn Vassily Vassilievich *(1643–1714), prince, statesman during the reign of Tsar Theodore and Tsarevna Sophia's regency*
Golovin Fyodor Alexeyevich *(1650–1706) count, admiral, first holder of the Order of St Andrew the First-Called, supervised Russian diplomacy during the reign of Peter the Great*

Irina Godunova, *tsarina, wife of Tsar Theodore and sister of Boris Godunov*

Ivan Danilovich Kalita *(?–1340), prince of Moscow (1325) and grand prince of Vladimir (1328)*

Ivan III *(1440–1505), mentioned in 1450 as co-ruler with his father, Basil the Blind, grand prince of Moscow (1462)*

Ivan IV (the Terrible) *(1530–1584), grand prince of Moscow (1533) and the first Russian tsar (1547)*

Ivan V *(1666–1696), son of Tsar Alexis, Russian tsar (1682) and co-ruler with Peter the Great*

Joachim *(1620–1690), Patriarch of All Russia (1674)*

Job *(?–1607), first Russian patriarch (1589–1605), protegé of Boris Godunov*

Jonah *(?–1470), Archbishop of Novgorod (1448), canonised in the 16th century*

Josaphat I, *Patriarch of Moscow (1634–1640), Philaret's successor*

Khitrovo Bogdan Matveyevich *(1615–1680), statesman and military figure, eminent boyar under Alexis and Theodore; founded the town of Simbirsk*

Khvorostinin Ivan Andreyevich *(?–1625), boyar, prince, voyevoda under Tsar Michael, author of a "chronicle" work on the Time of Troubles in Russia (the late 16th – early 17th century)*

Kutuzov Mikhail Illarionovich *(1745–1813), most radiant Prince of Smolensk (1812), Russian military leader, fieldmarshal (1812)*

Macarius *(1428–1563), Archbishop of Novgorod (1526), Metropolitan of Moscow and All Russia (1542), supervised the work of the One Hundred Chapters (Stoglav) assembly of the Russian church*

Maria Alexandrovna *(1824–1880) Empress, wife of Emperor Alexander II, née Maximiliana-Wilhelmina-Augusta-Sophia-Maria, daughter of Duke of Hessen-Darmstadt*

Maria Temriukovna, *second wife of Ivan the Terrible, Cabardinian princess*

Menshikov Alexander Danilovich *(1673–1729), Peter the Great's batman (1686), count (1702), most radiant prince (1707), generalissimus (1727)*

Michael Romanov *(1596–1645), first tsar of the Romanov dynasty, elected to the throne by the Assembly of the Land (1613)*

Michael, son of Yaroslav *(1271–1318), Prince of Tver (1285), grand prince of Vladimir (1305–1317)*

Moses *(?–1360), Archbishop of Novgorod, canonised in the 16th century*

Mstislavsky Fyodor Ivanovich *(?–1622), prince, boyar, voyevoda*

Nicholas I *(1796–1855), Russian Emperor (1825)*

Nicholas II *(1868–1918), the last Russian Emperor (1894–1917)*

Nikon *(1605–1681), churchman and politician, Russian patriarch (1652–1666)*

Orlov Grigory Grigorievich *(1734–1783), Russian military leader and politician, count (1762)*

Peter *(?–1326), Metropolitan of Russia. Moved the metropolitan see from Vladimir to Moscow, thereby ensuring the latter's ascendancy.*

Peter I (the Great) *(1672–1725), Russian tsar (1682), first Russian Emperor (1721), statesman and military leader*

Peter II *(1715–1730), grandson of Peter the Great and son of Tsarevich Alexis, Russian Emperor (1727)*

Philaret *(secular name Fyodor Nikitich Romanov) (c.1554/55–1633), Russian patriarch (1608–1610 and from 1619), father of Tsar Michael, boyar*

Philip *(1507–1569), Metropolitan of Moscow and All Russia (1566). Murdered on the orders of Ivan the Terrible*

Photius *(?–1431), Russian metropolitan (1409)*

Pitirim *(?–1673), Patriarch of All Russia (1672)*

Plato *(1737–1812), Russian metropolitan (1775), church writer and preacher, religious teacher of Catherine the Great's son Paul*

Platov Matvei Ivanovich *(1751–1818), leader of the Don Cossack host (1801), cavalry general (1809), count (1812), took part in the capture of Ochakov (1788) and Ismail (1790), hero of the war of 1812*

Potemkin Grigory Alexandrovich *(1739–1791), Russian statesman and military leader, diplomat, count (1770), most radiant prince of Tavrida (1783), field-marshal (1784)*

Pozharsky Dmitri Mikhailovich *(1578–1642), Russian statesman and military leader, prince, boyar (1613), popular hero*

Pseudo-Dmitri I *(?–1606), adventurist who claimed to be the Tsarevich Dmitri, Russian tsar (1605)*

Romanov Nikita Ivanovich *(?–1655), boyar (1646)*
Rumyantsev-Zadunaisky Pyotr Alexandrovich *(1725–1796), count (1744), Russian military commander and theoretician in the art of warfare, field-marshal (1770)*

Sergius of Radonezh *(c.1321–1391), churchman and politician, founder and later abbot of the Trinity Monastery near Moscow. Canonised in the 15th century*
Sheremetiev Fyodor Ivanovich *(?–1650), boyar, virtual head of the Russian government from 1642 to 1645*
Shuisky Pyotr-Guri Ivanovich *(?–1564), prince, voyevoda*
Sophia *(1657–1704), daughter of Tsar Alexis, ruler of the Russian state (1682–1689)*
Sophia (Zoya) Palaeologina, *niece of the last Byzantine emperor Constantine XI Palaelogus (1399–1453), second wife of Ivan III (1472), mother of Basil III*
Stroganov Grigory Dmitrievich *(1656–1715), in the 1690s united and extended the family land holdings in the Urals and Siberia. Gave considerable financial support to Peter the Great during the Northern War*
Suvorov Alexander Vassilievich *(1730–1800), military leader and theoretician, count of Rymnik (1789), prince Italiisky (1799), generalissimus (1799)*

Theodore, son of Ivan the Terrible *(1557–1598), last Russian tsar of the Riurikovich dynasty (1584)*

Ushakov Fyodor Fyodorovich *(1744 or 1745–1817), Russian naval commander, admiral (1799), one of the founders of the Black Sea fleet and its commander (1790)*

Vladimir Monomachus *(1053–1125), grand prince of Kiev (1113)*
Vorontsov Mikhail Semyonovich *(1782–1856), prince, statesman, field-marshal (1856), commander of the Russian occupation force in France (1815–1818), governor of Bessarabia (1823) and governor of the Caucasus (1844)*

Yaroslav II *(1191–1246), prince of Novgorod, grand prince of Vladimir (1238), the father of Alexander Nevsky*
Yaroslav the Wise *(c.978–1054), grand prince of Kiev (1019), the son of Prince Vladimir*
Yermak Timofeyevich *(?–1585), Cossack leader who served the Stroganovs, a family of industrialists in the Urals. Led a detachment equipped by him and routed the army of Khan Kuchum of Siberia (1582)*
Yuri (George) Dolgoruki *(1090s–1157), prince of Suzdal and grand prince of Kiev, the son of Vladimir Monomachus*